Maps Globes Graphs

Level D

Writer
Henry Billings

Consultants

Marian Gregory
Teacher
San Luis Coastal Unified School District
San Luis Obispo, California

Gloria Sesso
Supervisor of Social Studies
Half Hollow Hills School District
Dix Hills, New York

Norman McRae, Ph.D.
Former Director of Fine Arts and Social
Studies
Detroit Public Schools
Detroit, Michigan

Edna Whitfield
Former Social Studies Supervisor
St. Louis Public Schools
St. Louis, Missouri

Marilyn Nebenzahl
Social Studies Consultant
San Francisco, California

Karen Wiggins
Director of Social Studies
Richardson Independent School District
Richardson, Texas

Check the Maps•Globes•Graphs Website to find more fun geography activities at home.

Go to www.HarcourtAchieve.com/mggwelcome.html

⚓HarcourtAchieve

Rigby • Steck-Vaughn

www.HarcourtAchieve.com
1.800.531.5015

Acknowledgments

Cartography   Land Registration and Information Service
Amherst, Nova Scotia, Canada
Gary J. Robinson
MapQuest.com, Inc.
R.R. Donnelley and Sons Company
XNR Productions Inc., Madison, Wisconsin

Photography Credits
COVER (globe, clouds): © PhotoDisc; p. 4 © Patti McConville/The Image Bank; p. 5 (t) © PhotoDisc; p. 5 (b) © Rob Crandall/Stock Boston; pp. 6 (both), 7 (both) © PhotoDisc; p. 8 © Gordon R. Gainer/The Stock Market; p. 15 © Cenzus/FPG International; p. 75 (t) ©Aldo Brando/ Tony Stone Images; p. 75 (b) © Lena Rooraid/PhotoEdit.

Illustration Credits
Dennis Harms pp. 9, 15, 50, 51, 56 (both), 57 (both); Michael Krone pp. 29, 42; T.K. Riddle pp. 64, 68, 69; David Griffin pp. 65, 66, 67; Rusty Kaim p. 4

ISBN 0-7398-9104-9

© 2004 Harcourt Achieve Inc.

Contents

Geography Themes

In *Maps•Globes•Graphs* you will learn about some of the tools that scientists use to study **geography**. Geography is the study of Earth and the ways people live and work on Earth. Scientists use five themes, or main ideas, to help them organize information as they study geography.

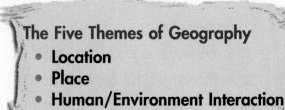

The Five Themes of Geography
- **Location**
- **Place**
- **Human/Environment Interaction**
- **Movement**
- **Regions**

Location

Location is where something can be found. One way to describe the location of something is by using numbers and a street name, or an address. Another way is by telling what the location is near.

Think about your home. Where is it located? What it is near? Think about the numbers and street name that make up your address.

This picture shows part of a crowded city. What makes it possible for mail to get to the right home or business?

Place

Place describes a location. Place tells about the **physical features** formed by nature, such as bodies of water, landforms, climate, and **natural resources**. Natural resources are things from nature that people can use. Some natural resources are trees, oil, and gold. Place also tells about the location's **human features**, or features made by people. Some examples of human features are buildings, roads, farms, schools and shopping malls.

 This picture shows Baltimore, Maryland. Look for physical and human features of Baltimore in the picture. Describe three features of Baltimore.

_____

_____

 Think about the features of your town or city. Describe three features of your town or city. Tell if they are physical or human features.

_____

_____

Human/Environment Interaction

Human/Environment Interaction describes how people live with their **environment**, or surroundings. The landforms, natural resources, and climate often determine how people live. For example, the kinds of food people eat often depends on their environment and what can grow there. Also, the houses people build and the jobs that they do often depend on the environment.

 How are the people who live in this house able to live at the edge of the ocean?

_____

_____

_____

Human/Environment Interaction also describes how people live in their environment by changing it. People might cut down trees to clear the land and build offices and other buildings.

Look at the pictures shown here. Why have people changed the environment in these places?

_____

_____

_____

_____

Movement

Movement describes how people, goods, information, and ideas move from place to place. Movement happens through transportation and communication.

People move in cars, buses, ships, trains, and planes. What are some ways goods move from place to place?

Information and ideas also move from place to place. This happens in newspapers, magazines, by telephone, and on radio and television.

🖉 Describe the kind of movement taking place in this picture.

_____

Regions

Regions are areas that share one or more features. A physical feature can describe a region. The Ohio River Valley is a physical landform region described by the Ohio River. Also, a human feature, such as how the land is used, can describe a region. Coal mining areas, such as those found in West Virginia and Kentucky form human land use regions because the land is used to mine natural resources. Regions can be as large as your state or as small as your neighborhood.

🖉 The Rocky Mountains run through Canada and the United States for more than 3,000 miles. What do you think makes the Rocky Mountains a region?

_____

_____

_____

_____

Directions and Legends

CARNIVAL

Look at the photograph shown here. The **title** of the photograph tells you what you are looking at. The title has large dark print.

A **compass rose** helps you find directions. Find the compass rose at the bottom of the photograph. A compass rose always tells you which way is north (N). Find the arrows pointing to south (S), east (E), and west (W). These are four **cardinal directions.**

► In which direction on the photograph do you look to find the giraffe bounce?

► In which direction on the photograph do you look to find the slide?

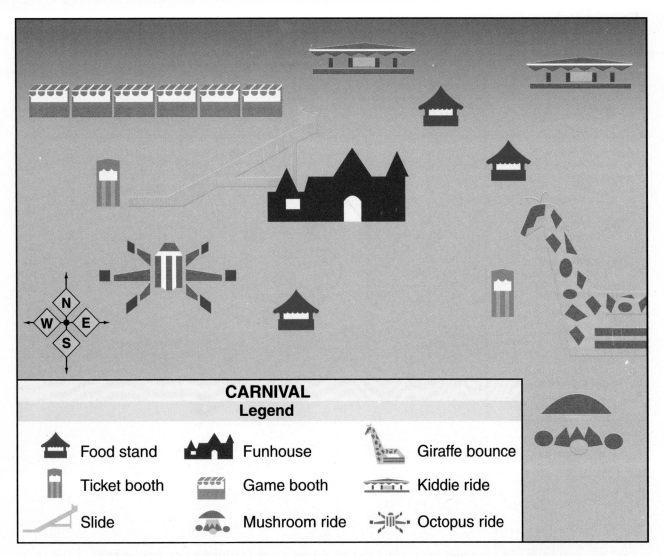

CARNIVAL
Legend

🏠 Food stand	🏰 Funhouse	🦒 Giraffe bounce
Ticket booth	Game booth	Kiddie ride
Slide	Mushroom ride	Octopus ride

This is a **map** of the photograph on page 8. A map is a drawing of a real place. On a map **symbols** stand for real things. To know what map symbols mean, you need to read the **map key** or **legend**. Find the symbol for funhouse in the legend and locate it on the map. Can you find the funhouse in the photograph on page 8?

► Compare the photograph and the map. What do you see in both the photograph and the map?

► Is there anything in the photograph that is not on the map?

► Why do you think some things are not on the map?

Most maps have a compass rose to show directions. Find the compass rose on this map.

► What direction is it from the giraffe bounce to the octopus ride?

► What direction is it from the mushroom ride to the giraffe bounce?

► What direction do you walk if you go from the game booths to the slide?

Reading a Resource Map

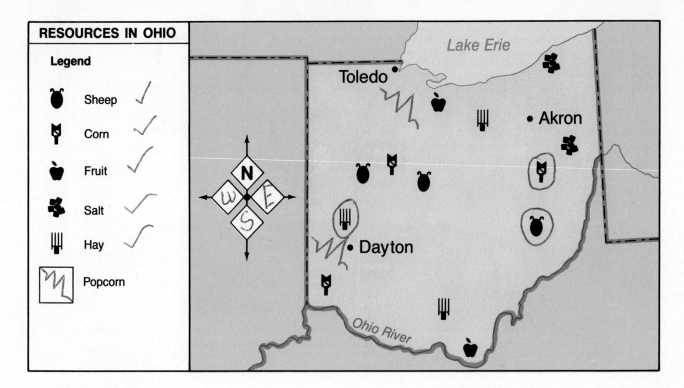

RESOURCES IN OHIO

Legend

🐑 Sheep ✓

🌽 Corn ✓

🍎 Fruit ✓

✦ Salt ✓

🌾 Hay ✓

〰 Popcorn

Lake Erie

Toledo

• Akron

N W E S

• Dayton

Ohio River

Resources are things that people can use. Symbols on this map stand for resources in the state of Ohio. Follow these map attack steps to read the map.

MAP ATTACK!

- **Read the title.** This map shows _Resources in Ohio_
- **Read the legend.** Check (✔) each symbol as you read its meaning. Then check (✔) a matching symbol on the map.
- **Read the compass rose.** Circle the north arrow. Label the other three arrows.

1. Find a symbol for corn south of Akron. Circle it.
2. Find a symbol for hay north of Dayton. Circle it.
3. Find a symbol for sheep east of Dayton. Circle it.
4. Draw a symbol for popcorn in the legend where it belongs.
5. Draw two popcorn symbols. Draw one south of Toledo, and one west of Dayton.

6. What resource is found only in eastern Ohio? _salt_

7. What resource is found only in western Ohio? _Popcorn_

Reading a Population Map

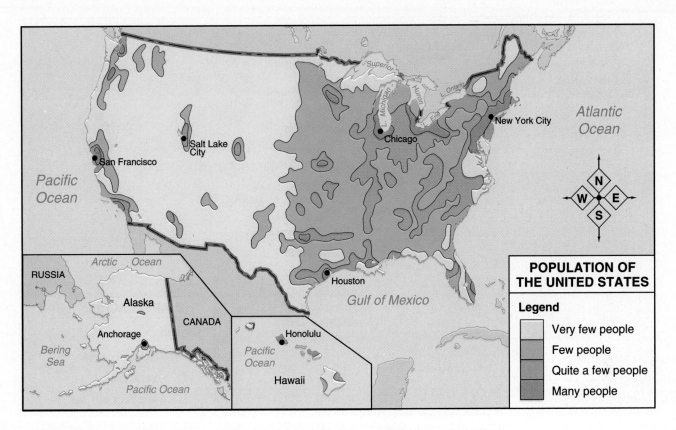

Population is the number of people who live in a place. Look at the population map above. It shows you how many people live in different areas of the United States.

1. Which color shows that many people live in an area?

   Brown

2. Find the area where you live on the map. What color is your area?

   Brown

3. Find Houston on the map. Do <u>many</u> or <u>very few</u> people live there?

   Many

4. Find Chicago on the map. Do <u>many</u> or <u>few</u> people live there?

   Many

5. Why do you think people want to live in these areas of our country?

   There Big

Reading Symbols on a Map

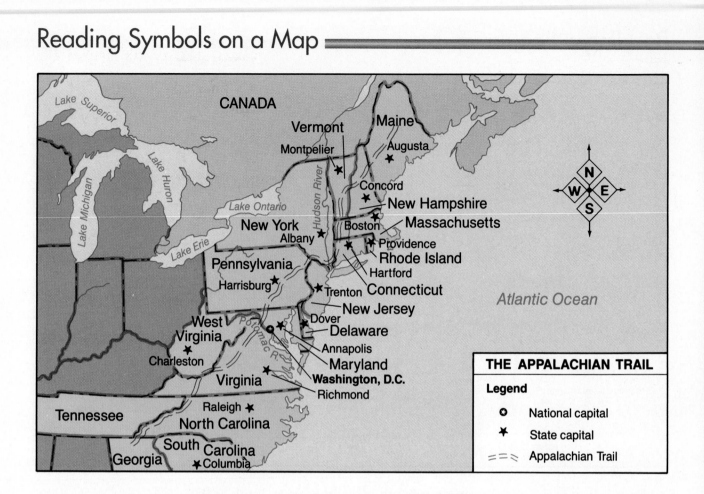

The Appalachian Trail is a hiking path in the eastern United States. It stretches through many different states. The Trail is over 2,000 miles long.

1. The northern end of the Appalachian Trail is in what state?

   Maine

2. The southern end of the Appalachian Trail is in what state?

   Georgia

3. Which state capital is closest to the trail?

   Harris Burg

4. Which river crosses the Appalachian Trail and runs through our

   national capital? _Potomac_

5. Name two states that are completely east of the Appalachian Trail.

   Rhode Island and _South Carolina_

6. The trail crosses the Hudson River in what state?

   New York

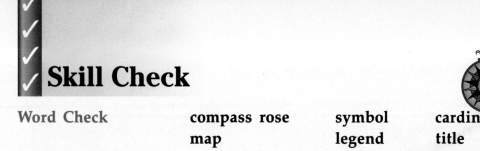

Skill Check

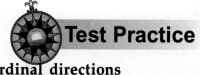

Word Check   compass rose   symbol   cardinal directions

                               map   legend   title

Write each word or phrase above in a sentence.

1. A _____ is a drawing of a real place.

2. A _____ stands for something real.

3. The _____ explains what the map's symbols mean.

4. The _____ helps you find directions on a map.

5. The letters N, S, E, and W stand for _____ .

Map Check

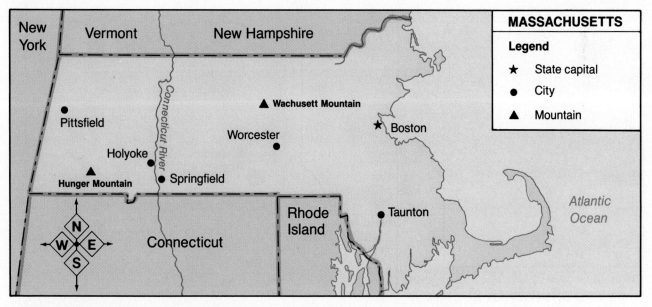

Find each place described below on the map. Write its name in the space provided.

1. A mountain west of Holyoke. _____

2. A city south of Wachusett Mountain. _____

3. A city along the eastern side of the Connecticut River.

_____

4. A city along the western side of the Connecticut River.

_____

Intermediate Directions

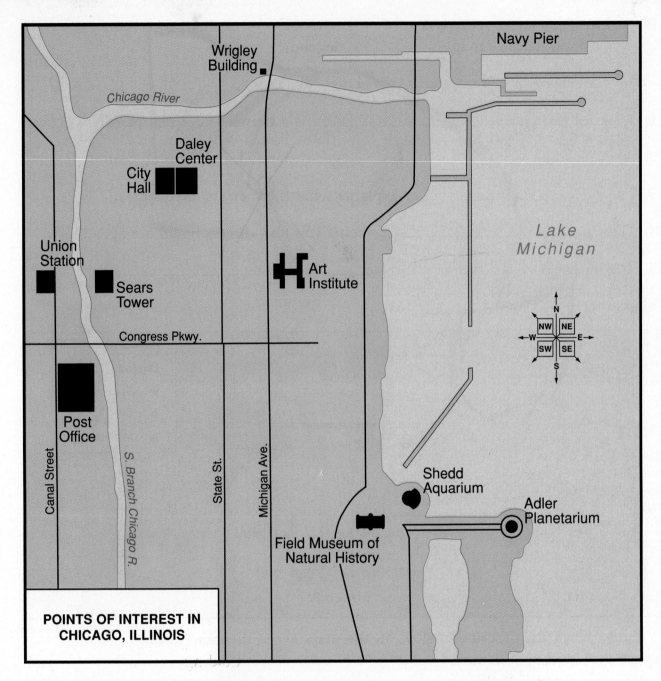

POINTS OF INTEREST IN
CHICAGO, ILLINOIS

You already know about the cardinal directions—north, south, east, and west. We use the cardinal directions to find places on Earth.

Look at the map above. Suppose you are at the Field Museum of Natural History in Chicago. Find it on the map. To get to the Adler Planetarium you go east.

You decide to walk from the Museum of Natural History to the Union Station. Find Union Station on the map. Are you walking north? Are you walking west? You are walking between north and west. That direction is called northwest.

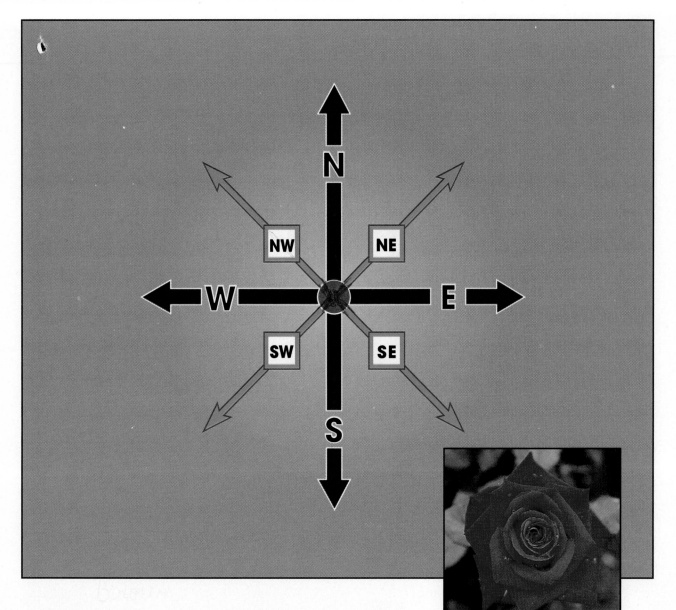

Northeast (NE), southeast (SE), southwest (SW), and northwest (NW) are **intermediate directions**. Look at the compass rose above. Find the arrows for north, east, south, and west. Then find the "in-between" arrows. These arrows point to the intermediate directions. Notice how the compass rose looks like an unfolding flower.

You can practice finding intermediate directions every time you read a compass rose. Practice now on the map on page 14.

► From the Field Museum of Natural History, which direction is each of these places?

                Daley Center   Navy Pier   Sears Tower

► Find City Hall on the map. Which direction would you walk to get to each of these places?

                Union Station   Art Institute   Wrigley Building

Using Intermediate Directions

ILLINOIS

Legend
★ State capital
● City or Town

MAP ATTACK!

● **Read the title.** This map shows _____.
● **Read the compass rose.** Label the intermediate direction arrows.
  Use NE for northeast, SE for southeast, SW for southwest, and NW
  for northwest.

Write the best intermediate direction in each sentence.

1. Find Springfield, the capital of Illinois. Circle it.
   Draw a line from Springfield to Bloomington.

   Bloomington is _____NE_____ of Springfield.

2. Draw a line from Springfield to Alton.

   Alton is _____SW_____ of Springfield.

3. Draw a line from Springfield to Flora.

   Flora is _____SE_____ of Springfield.

4. Draw a line from Springfield to Macomb.

   Macomb is _____NW_____ of Springfield.

Using Intermediate Directions

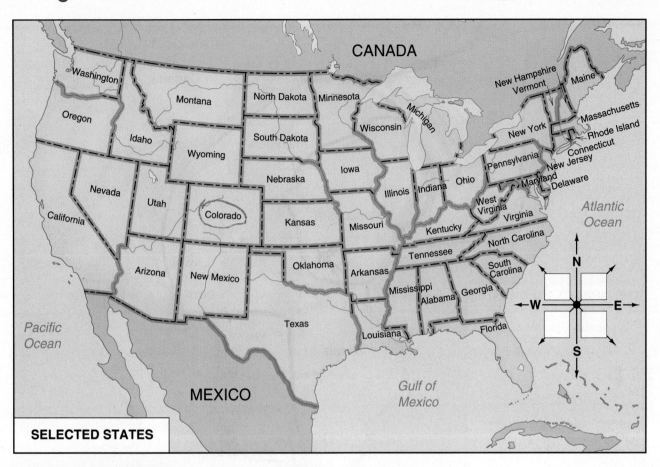

MAP ATTACK!

Follow the steps on page 16 to begin reading this map.

1. Find Colorado on the map. Circle the label.

   a. Which state is to the northeast of Colorado? _Nebraska_

   b. Which state is to the southeast of Colorado? _Oklahoma_

   c. Which state is to the southwest of Colorado? _Arizona_

   d. Which state is to the northwest of Colorado? _Wyoming_

2. Find each state below. In which part of the United States is it located?
   Write NE, SE, SW, or NW.

   a. Arizona _SW_   b. New York _NE_   c. Massachusetts _NE_

   d. Georgia _SE_   e. Oregon _NW_   f. South Carolina _SE_

   g. New Jersey _NE_   h. Florida _SE_   i. Pennsylvania _NE_

Directions in the Great Lakes States

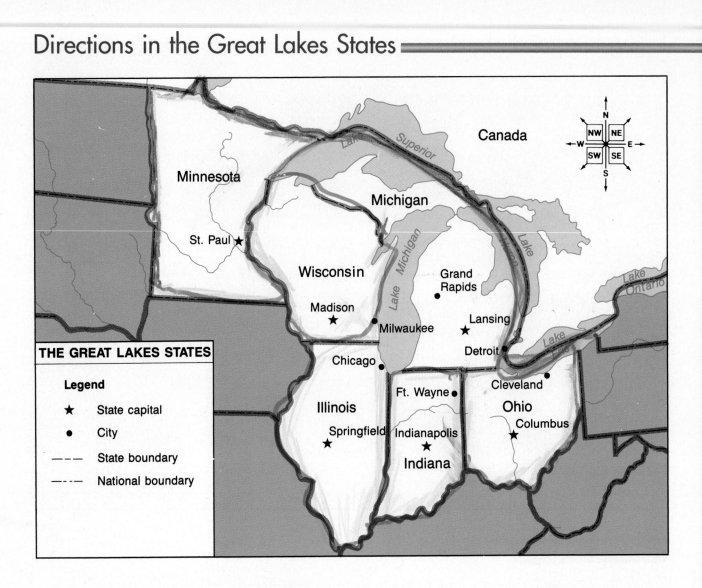

1. Trace the state boundaries in green.
2. Trace the national boundary in red.
3. Color the states yellow.
   Choose another light color and color Canada.
4. Find each place below on the map. Write the direction you would travel from the first place to the second place. Use cardinal and intermediate directions. The first one is done for you.

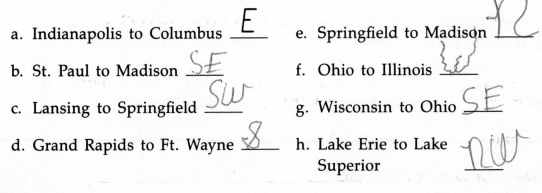

a. Indianapolis to Columbus __E__   e. Springfield to Madison __N__

b. St. Paul to Madison __SE__   f. Ohio to Illinois __W__

c. Lansing to Springfield __SW__   g. Wisconsin to Ohio __SE__

d. Grand Rapids to Ft. Wayne __S__   h. Lake Erie to Lake __NW__
   Superior

Skill Check

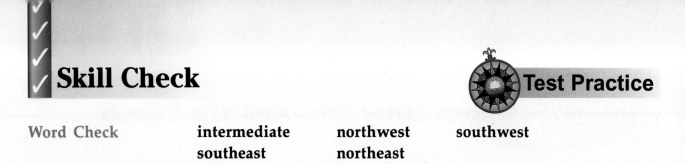

Word Check   **intermediate   northwest   southwest   southeast   northeast**

1. Finish the compass rose on the map below. Add the intermediate directions NE, SE, SW, and NW.

2. _____ directions are between the cardinal directions.

Map Check

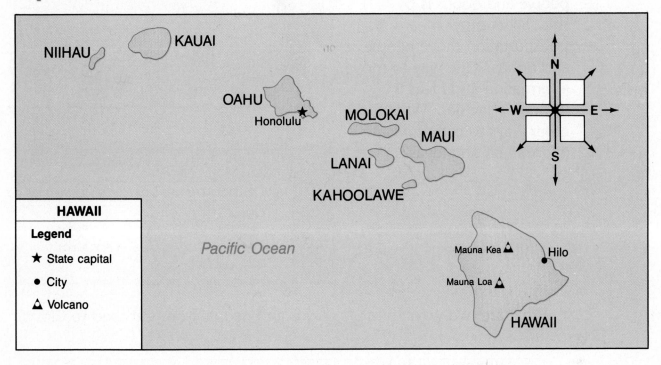

1. Find the island of Lanai on the map. Circle it.
2. Draw a line from Lanai to Maui.

   Maui is _____ of Lanai.
3. Draw a line from Lanai to the big island of Hawaii.

   Hawaii is _____ of Lanai.
4. Draw a line from Lanai to Oahu.

   Oahu is _____ of Lanai.
5. Find the city of Hilo on the big island of Hawaii.

   Which volcano is southwest of Hilo? _____

   Which volcano is northwest of Hilo? _____

Geography Themes Up Close

Movement tells how people, goods, information, and ideas move from place to place. Transportation and communication demonstrate movement. One way to move people and goods is by ship. What other means of transportation move people and goods? One way to move information and ideas is through television. What are other ways to communicate information and ideas?

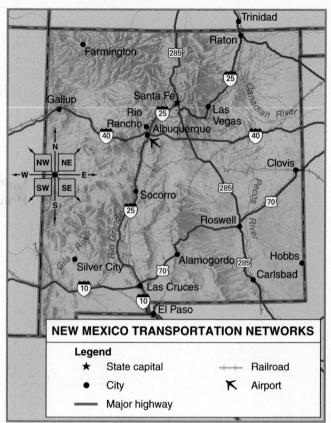

NEW MEXICO TRANSPORTATION NETWORKS

Legend
★ State capital
● City
▬▬ Major highway
┼┼┼ Railroad
✠ Airport

1. What are two ways to move goods and people from Carlsbad to Clovis?

   _____

2. What city is the center of transportation in New Mexico? Why do you think this is so?

   _____

   _____

3. Trace the shortest driving route from Las Cruces to Santa Fe. What highway would you take from Las Cruces to Santa Fe?

   _____

4. What cities would you pass through between Las Cruces and Santa Fe?

   _____

5. New Mexico needs another airport. Put an **X** on the map where you think an airport should be built. Explain why you think this is a good location for an airport.

_____

_____

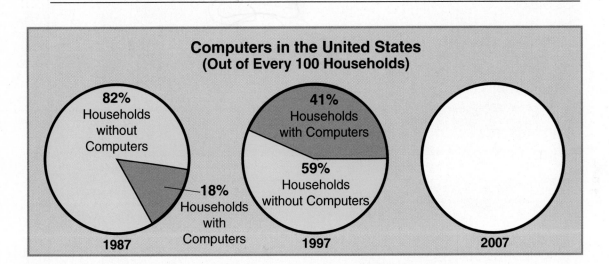

Computers in the United States
(Out of Every 100 Households)

82% Households without Computers

18% Households with Computers

1987

41% Households with Computers

59% Households without Computers

1997

2007

Computers move information and ideas throughout the United States and the world. The first two circle graphs show the number of households (out of every 100 households) in the United States that have computers.

6. Out of every 100 households in 1987, how many had computers?

_____

7. Out of every 100 households in 1997, how many had computers? Is this number more or less than in 1987?

_____

8. Predict how many households out of every 100 in the United States will have a computer in 2007. Complete the circle graph for 2007 with the number you predict. Explain your prediction.

_____

_____

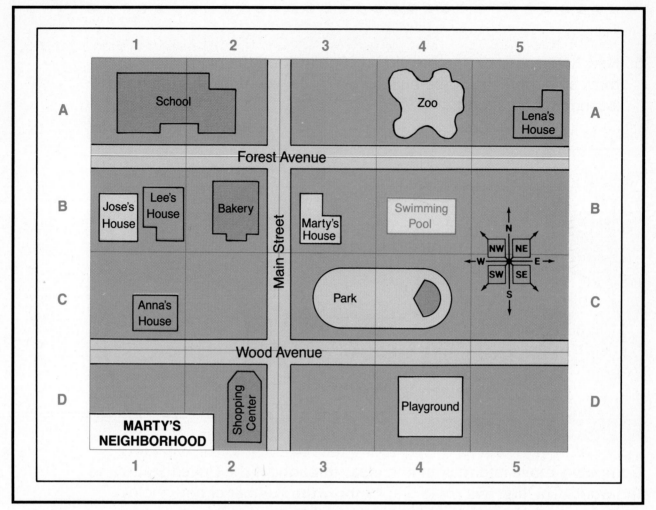

A **grid** is a pattern of lines drawn on a map to help you find places. We label the rows on a grid with letters. We label the columns with numbers. Find the letters along each side of the map above. Now find the numbers across the top and bottom. Do you see the squares on the map?

Locate Marty's house on the map above. It is in square B-3. Find the letter B on the left side of the map. Slide your finger across row B until you reach column 3. You are now in square B-3.

► Which building is located in the square to the west of B-3? What is the name of this square?

► The zoo is located in square A-4. Find it on your map. Where could you go if you walked south one square? What is the name of this square?

► Anna rode her bike to the shopping center. It is in square D-2. Find it on your map. Later she will meet Marty at the bakery. The bakery is in square B-2. Which direction should she bike to reach the bakery?

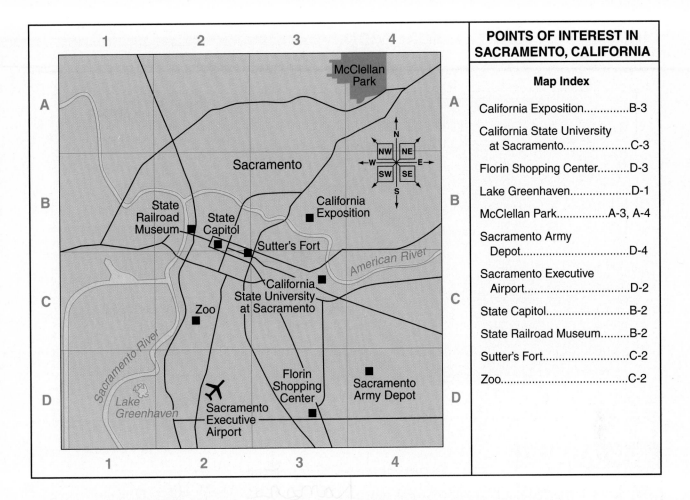

POINTS OF INTEREST IN SACRAMENTO, CALIFORNIA

Map Index

California Exposition..............B-3

California State University
   at Sacramento....................C-3

Florin Shopping Center..........D-3

Lake Greenhaven...................D-1

McClellan Park................A-3, A-4

Sacramento Army
   Depot..............................D-4

Sacramento Executive
   Airport...............................D-2

State Capitol.........................B-2

State Railroad Museum.........B-2

Sutter's Fort...........................C-2

Zoo..C-2

You can find a place on a map grid by looking it up in the map index. A **map index** is an alphabetical list of the places on the map. A map index lists each place with the letter and number of its grid square.

Look at the map on this page. It shows places of interest in Sacramento, California. To find places on the map, you use the map index. Suppose you want to visit the zoo. Look up "zoo" in the map index. The map index tells you that the zoo is in square C-2. To find this square on the map, put your finger on the C and slide it across row C until you reach column 2. This is square C-2. You can now find the zoo.

► Use the map index to find Lake Greenhaven. In which grid square is it located? Find Lake Greenhaven on the map.

► Look up Florin Shopping Center in the map index. In which grid square is it located? Find Florin Shopping Center on the map.

► Locate Sutter's Fort using the map index. In which grid square is it located? Find it on the map. Name two other points of interest located in this same square.

► Use the map index to find McClellan Park. Now find the Sacramento Army Depot. Which direction would you travel to get from McClellan Park to the Sacramento Army Depot?

Finding Places on a State Map

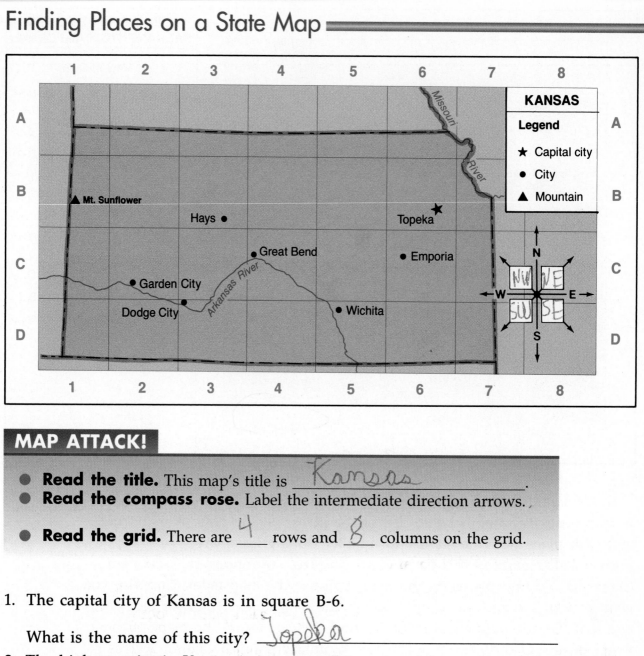

MAP ATTACK!

- **Read the title.** This map's title is _Kansas_.
- **Read the compass rose.** Label the intermediate direction arrows.
- **Read the grid.** There are _4_ rows and _8_ columns on the grid.

1. The capital city of Kansas is in square B-6.

   What is the name of this city? _Topeka_

2. The highest point in Kansas is in square B-1.

   What is the name of this mountain? _Mt. Sunflower_

3. The largest city in Kansas is in square D-5.

   What is the name of this city? _Witchita_

4. Great Bend is a city in square C-4. Locate it on your map.

   This city is on which river? _arkansas_

5. Name two other cities on the Arkansas River. Then write the letter and number of their grid squares.

   Dodge City D2, Garden City c2, Witchita D5

Finding Places on a Regional Map

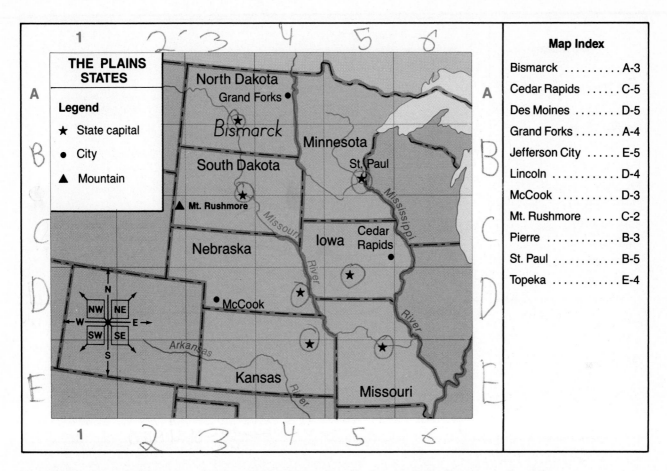

THE PLAINS STATES

Legend
★ State capital
● City
▲ Mountain

Map Index

Bismarck	A-3
Cedar Rapids	C-5
Des Moines	D-5
Grand Forks	A-4
Jefferson City	E-5
Lincoln	D-4
McCook	D-3
Mt. Rushmore	C-2
Pierre	B-3
St. Paul	B-5
Topeka	E-4

1. Finish the map grid. Write the letters B, C, D, and E down each side of the map. Write the numbers 2, 3, 4, 5, and 6 across the top and bottom of the map. The first letter and number are done for you.

2. Use the index to find the places listed below. Circle each one on the map. Then write the name of the state where each place is located.

    Mt. Rushmore _South Dakota_ Cedar Rapids _Iowa_

    McCook _Nebraska_ Grand Forks _North Dakota_

3. Use the index to locate each state capital listed below. Write the name of each state capital where it belongs on the map. Then write the name of the state where each capital is located. The first one is done for you.

    Bismarck _North Dakota_ Des Moines _Iowa_

    Jefferson City _Missouri_ Lincoln _Nebraska_

    Pierre _South Dakota_ Topeka _Kansas_

Finding Places in Yellowstone National Park

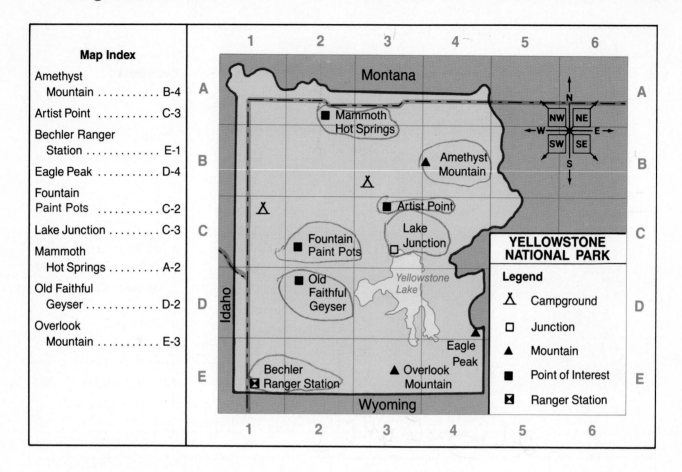

Map Index

Amethyst
   Mountain B-4

Artist Point C-3

Bechler Ranger
   Station E-1

Eagle Peak D-4

Fountain
Paint Pots C-2

Lake Junction C-3

Mammoth
   Hot Springs A-2

Old Faithful
   Geyser D-2

Overlook
   Mountain E-3

1. Use the map index to find each place on the map.
   Draw a circle around each place.

      Old Faithful Geyser   Mammoth Hot Springs
      Lake Junction   Fountain Paintpots
      Bechler Ranger Station   Amethyst Mountain

2. Find Artist Point on the map. Draw a circle around it.
   Write the direction you would travel from Artist Point to each place
   below. The first one is done for you.

   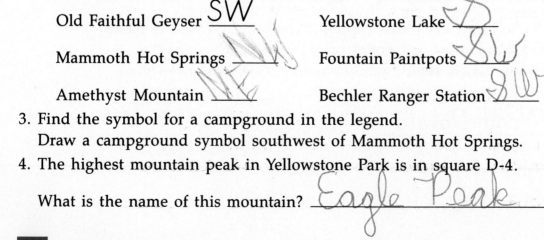

   Old Faithful Geyser SW   Yellowstone Lake _____

   Mammoth Hot Springs _____   Fountain Paintpots _____

   Amethyst Mountain _____   Bechler Ranger Station _____

3. Find the symbol for a campground in the legend.
   Draw a campground symbol southwest of Mammoth Hot Springs.

4. The highest mountain peak in Yellowstone Park is in square D-4.

   What is the name of this mountain? _Eagle Peak_____

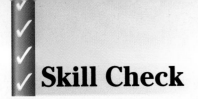

Skill Check

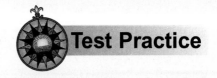

Word Check   **grid**   **index**

1. A map _____ lists places found on a map. It is arranged in alphabetical order.

2. A _____ is a pattern of crossing lines that make rows and columns on a map.

Map Check

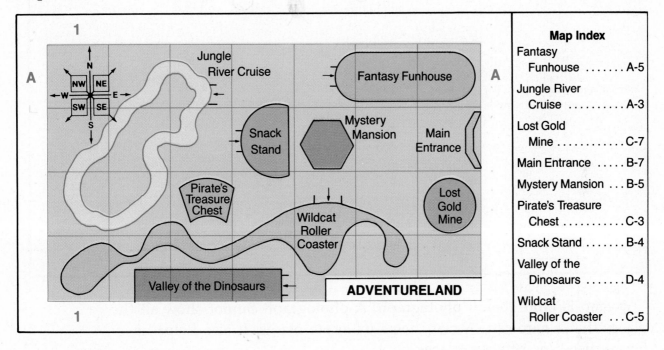

1. Finish the map grid. Label each row with a letter and each column with a number. The first ones are done for you.

2. Use the map index to find Mystery Mansion.

   In which square is it located? _____
   Find it on your map and draw a circle around it.

3. In which square is the Pirate's Treasure Chest located? _____
   Write the direction you would walk from Mystery Mansion to the

   Pirate's Treasure Chest. _____

4. In which square is the Lost Gold Mine located? _____
   Write the direction you would walk from Mystery Mansion to the

   Lost Gold Mine. _____

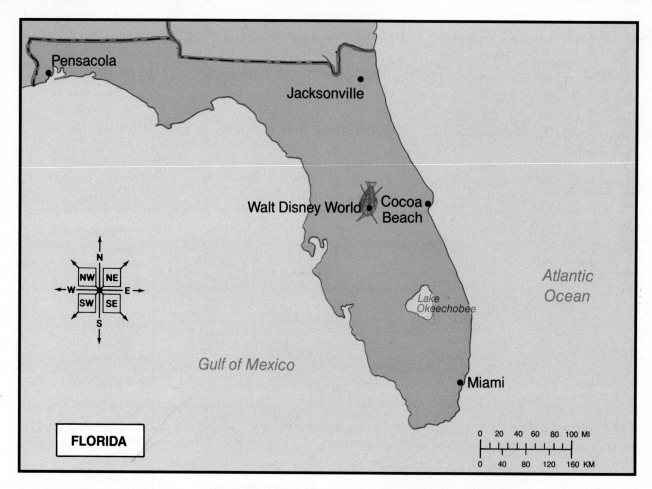

A map is more than a photograph. A photograph cannot show all the places that a map can. A map helps us locate places. It also helps us figure distances between places.

Florida is 450 miles long. A map cannot be that long! We must make maps small enough to hold. So on this map of Florida, one inch equals one hundred miles.

How do we know that? We find out that one inch equals one hundred miles by reading the **map scale**. A map scale looks like this:

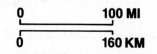

The marks and numbers along the top stand for distance in miles. The marks and numbers along the bottom stand for distance in kilometers. **Miles** and **kilometers** are two ways of measuring distance.

► Find the map scale on the map above.

What letters stand for <u>miles</u>?

What letters stand for <u>kilometers</u>?

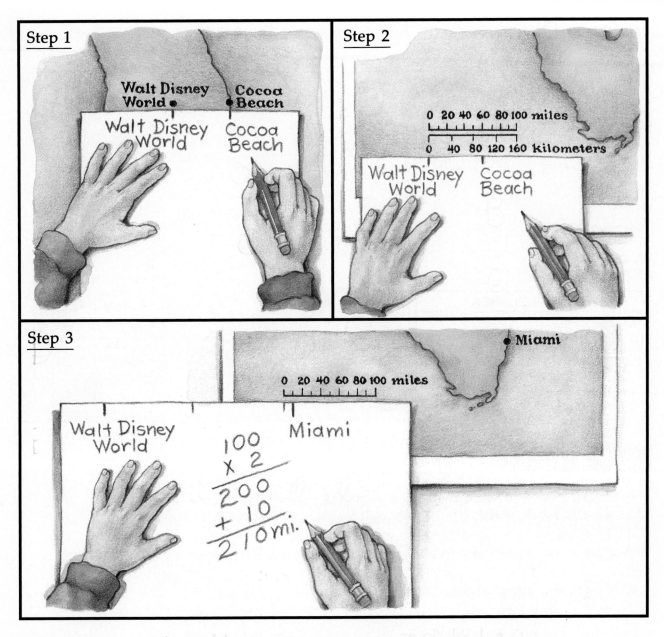

You are on vacation in Florida. You want to find the distance between Walt Disney World and Cocoa Beach. Here's how you use the map scale.

Step 1 Place the edge of a piece of paper in a straight line from Walt Disney World to Cocoa Beach. Mark your paper below each city.

Step 2 Lay the edge of your paper along the scale. Your left-hand mark should be below "0". Read the scale numbers nearest your right-hand mark. The numbers tell you that Walt Disney World and Cocoa Beach are 60 miles apart.

Step 3 What if the distance is more than 100 miles? Find out how many times the scale fits between your two marks. Multiply the number of times it fits by the high number on the scale. Then add the extra amount.

▶ How many miles apart are Walt Disney World and Miami?

Figuring Distance on a Map

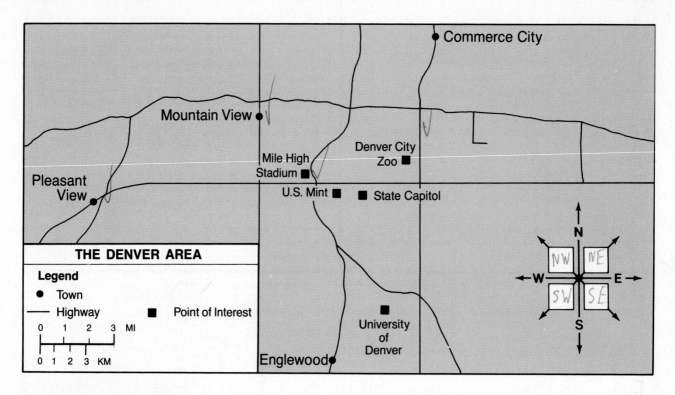

MAP ATTACK!

- **Read the title.** This map shows ___The Denver Area___ .
- **Read the legend.** Check (✔) each symbol as you read its meaning. Then check (✔) a matching symbol on the map.
- **Read the compass rose.** Label the intermediate direction arrows.
- **Read the map scale.** The scale goes up to __3__ miles.

Use the map scale and the edge of a piece of paper to figure these distances. Write the distance in miles for questions 1 through 4. Write the distance in kilometers for question 5.

1. From the University of Denver to Mile High Stadium is about __6__ miles.

2. From the Denver City Zoo to Englewood is about __8__ miles.

3. From the State Capitol to the University of Denver is about __5__ miles.

4. From the U.S. Mint to Commerce City is about __7 ½__ miles.

5. From Pleasant View to Mountain View is about __8__ kilometers.

Figuring Distances on a Map

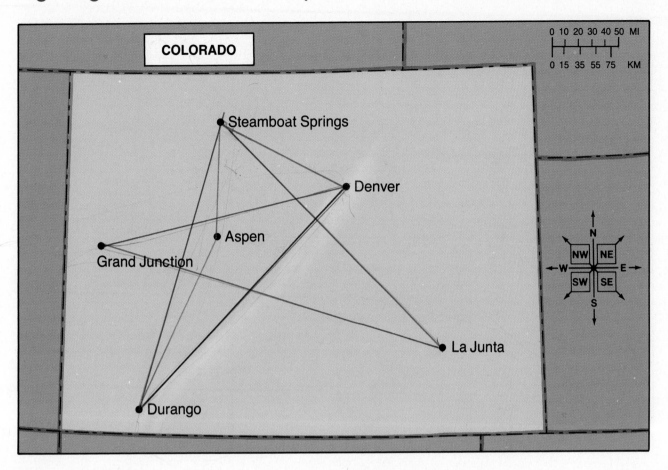

You are about to go on a flying trip through the Rocky Mountains. Your plane will land in several cities. How many miles will you travel?

Use the map scale and the edge of a piece of paper to figure the distance.

1. Draw a line from Denver to Durango.

   Measure the distance from Denver to Durango. __225__ miles ✓✓✓

2. Draw a line from Durango to Aspen.

   Measure the distance from Durango to Aspen. __140__ miles ✓✓✓

3. Draw a line from Aspen to Steamboat Springs.

   Measure the distance from Aspen to Steamboat Springs. __88__ miles ✓✓

4. Draw a line from Steamboat Springs to Denver.

   Measure the distance from Steamboat Springs to Denver. __105__ miles ✓✓

5. How many miles did you fly? Add the number of miles between each city. The total distance of your trip was __558__ miles.

Figuring Distance in the Mountain States

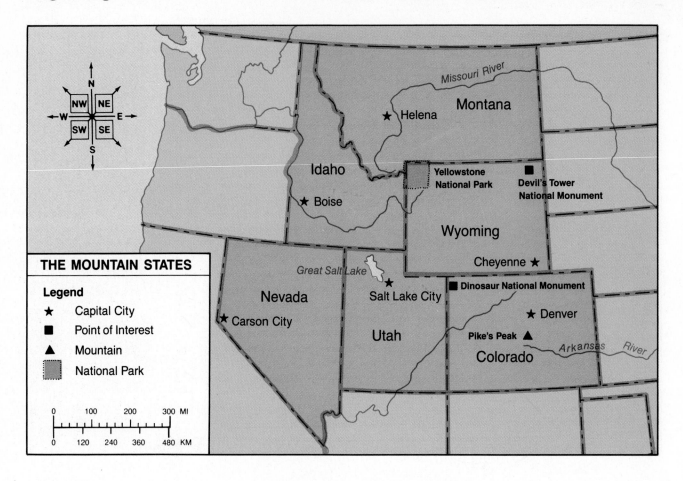

You and your family are planning a trip through the mountain states. Below is the daily log you need to complete before the trip. Finish the daily log. The first day is done for you.

Day 1   Drive from Yellowstone National Park to Devil's Tower.

Drive _____ east _____ for about _____ 260 _____ miles.

Day 2   Drive from Devil's Tower to Dinosaur National Monument.

Drive _South West_ for about ___350___ miles.

Day 3   Drive from Dinosaur National Monument to Pike's Peak.

Drive _South East_ for about ___230___ miles.

Day 4   Drive from Pike's Peak to Cheyenne.

Drive _____North_____ for about ___290___ miles.

Day 5   Drive from Cheyenne to Yellowstone National Park.

Drive _North West_ for about ___344___ miles.

Skill Check

Word Check   **map scale**   **kilometers**   **miles**

Write each word in a sentence.

1. Two ways of measuring distance on Earth are _____

   and _____ .

2. A _____ helps us measure distance on a map.

Map Check

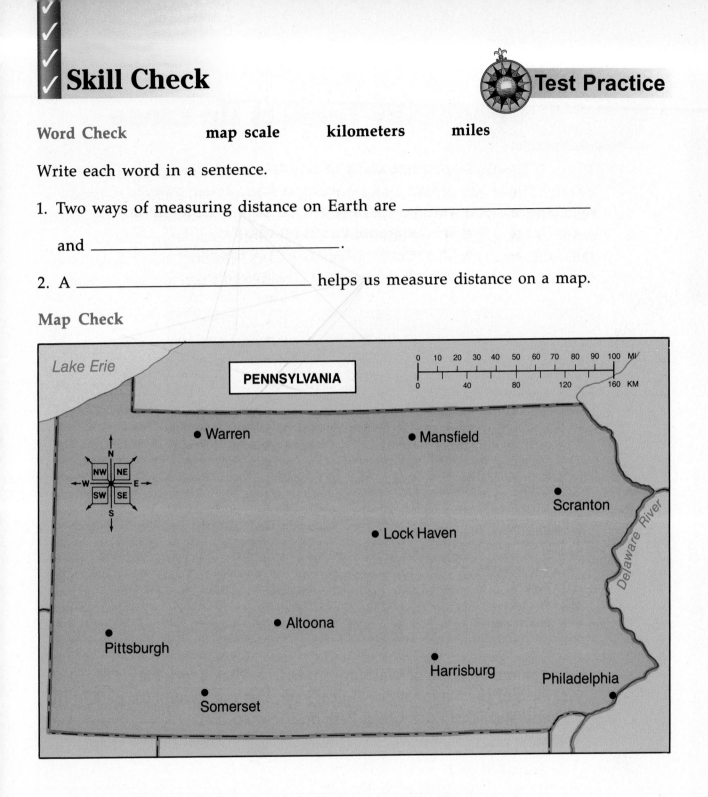

Use the map scale and a piece of paper to find these distances.

1. Somerset is about _____ miles from Altoona.

2. Mansfield is about _____ miles from Scranton.

3. Harrisburg is about _____ miles from Warren.

4. Altoona is about _____ miles from Pittsburgh.

Geography Themes Up Close

Place is a location that has physical and human features that make it different from any other location. Physical features can include natural resources, bodies of water, and plants and animals. Human features, those made by people, can include parks, playgrounds, buildings, bridges, railroads, and factories. The map below shows Washington, D.C. Look at the features that make Washington, D.C. different from any other place.

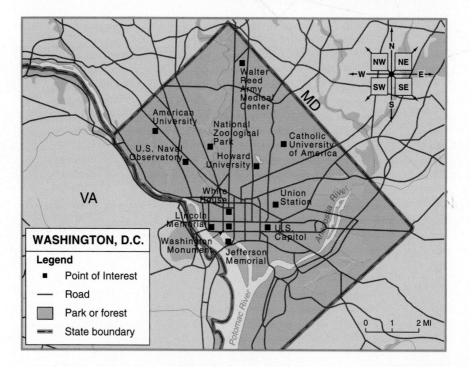

1. One human feature of Washington, D.C. is Rock Creek Park. This park is north of the National Zoological Park. Use the symbol for park in the legend and label Rock Creek Park on the map.

2. Name a physical feature of Washington, D.C. shown on the map.

_____

3. Find the U.S. Capitol on the map. It is southeast of the White House. Circle the U.S. Capitol. Write **P** next to it if it is a physical feature; write **H** if it is a human feature.

4. What are two other human features of Washington, D.C. shown on the map?

_____

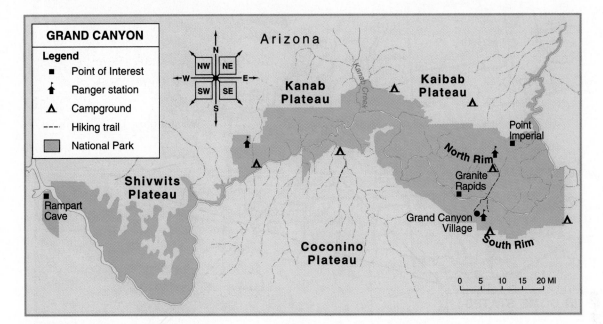

GRAND CANYON

Legend
- ■ Point of Interest
- ⬧ Ranger station
- ⛺ Campground
- --- Hiking trail
- ▨ National Park

Arizona

Kanab Plateau

Kaibab Plateau

Point Imperial

North Rim

Granite Rapids

Grand Canyon Village

South Rim

Shivwits Plateau

Rampart Cave

Coconino Plateau

0   5   10   15   20 MI

5. Label the Colorado River on the map. Write **P** next to it if it is a physical feature; write **H** if it is a human feature.

6. What are two other physical features of the Grand Canyon?

_____

7. The Grand Canyon Village is a human feature of the Grand Canyon. It is in the southeastern part of the Grand Canyon. Circle the Grand Canyon Village.

8. What are two other human features of the Grand Canyon?

_____

9. Describe how the features of the Grand Canyon differ from the features of Washington, D.C.

_____

_____

_____

_____

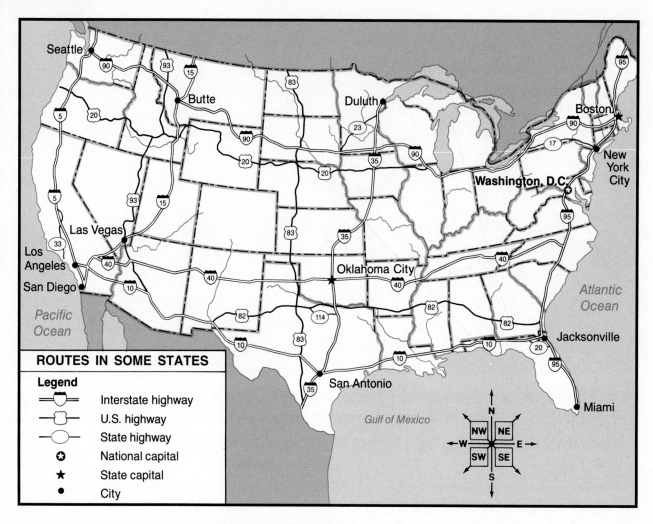

A **route** is a way of getting from one place to another. This route map shows highways in the United States. The legend shows different highway symbols used on the map. Highways are named with numbers.

Three kinds of highways are shown on this map.

Interstate highway: a main highway with many lanes. Interstate highways often cross the entire country from east to west or from north to south.

U.S. highway: a main highway that passes through more than one state.

State highway: a main road that connects cities and towns within the boundaries of one state.

► Find each highway in the legend and on the map.

► What interstate highways run north and south on the map?

► What interstate highways run east and west on the map?

► What U.S. highways can you find on the map?

► What state highways can you find on the map?

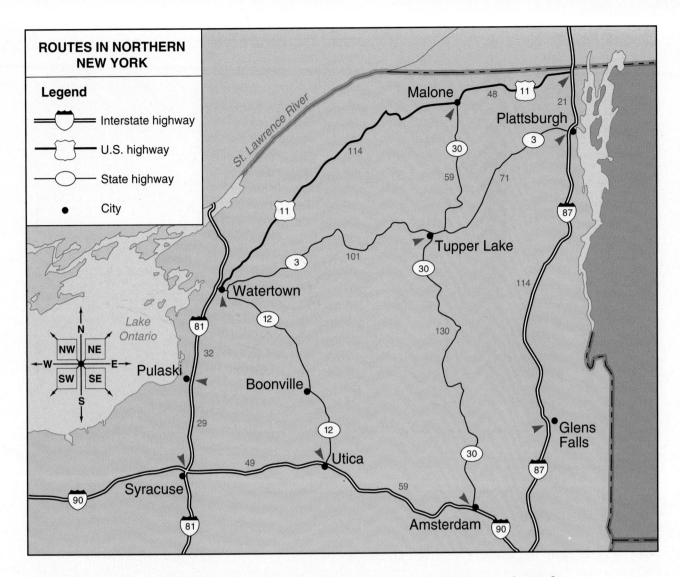

ROUTES IN NORTHERN NEW YORK

Legend

Interstate highway
U.S. highway
State highway
• City

Route maps can help you find the distances between places. Look at the map above. Find the cities of Syracuse and Utica. Do you see the small red triangles pointing to each city? Now find the red number 49 between the triangles. This number tells you that there are 49 miles between the triangles. You now know that Syracuse and Utica are 49 miles apart.

► How many miles apart are Utica and Amsterdam?

► How many miles apart are Amsterdam and Tupper Lake?

► How many miles apart are Plattsburgh and Glens Falls?

Sometimes you must add the red numbers to find out the total distance between places. Imagine that you are driving from Pulaski to Plattsburgh. To find out how far you will drive, answer these questions.

► How many miles is it from Pulaski to Watertown?

► How many miles is it from Watertown to Tupper Lake?

► How many miles is it from Tupper Lake to Plattsburgh?

► Now add up the numbers to find the distance from Pulaski to Plattsburgh.

Reading a Route Map

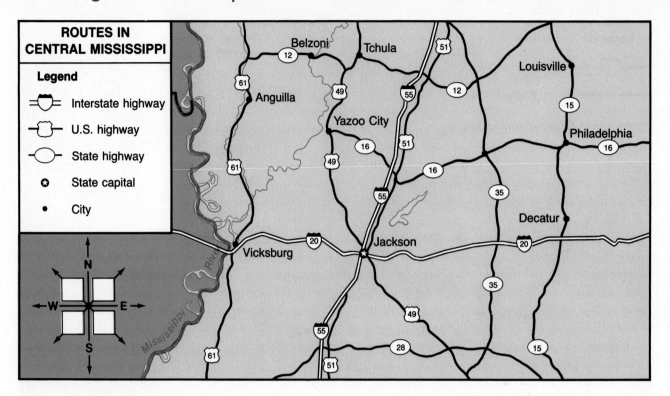

ROUTES IN CENTRAL MISSISSIPPI

Legend
- Interstate highway
- U.S. highway
- State highway
- ✪ State capital
- • City

MAP ATTACK!

● **Read the title.** This map shows _____.

● **Read the legend.** The three routes shown are _____

_____.

● **Read the compass rose.** Label the intermediate direction arrows.

1. What highway crosses the Mississippi River? _____

2. What highway enters Vicksburg from the north? _____

3. What U.S. highway goes through Jackson? _____

4. What other cities does that route go through? _____

_____

5. Find the city where highways 16 and 35 meet.
   Label that city <u>Carthage</u>.

6. What U.S. highway goes alongside Interstate 55? _____

Reading a Route Map

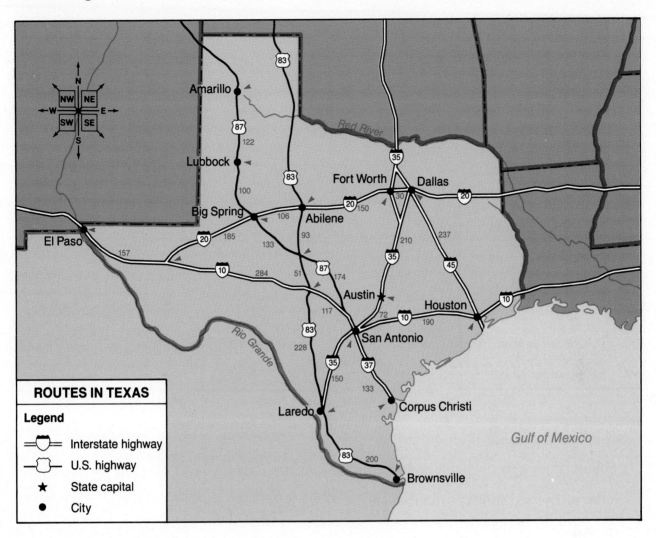

ROUTES IN TEXAS

Legend

- ⬭ Interstate highway
- ⬭ U.S. highway
- ★ State capital
- ● City

1. What does this map show? _____
2. Read the red mileage numbers between the cities below. Write the distances.

   Austin to San Antonio _____   Abilene to Fort Worth _____

   Laredo to Brownsville _____   Dallas to Houston _____

   Amarillo to Lubbock _____   San Antonio to Corpus Christi _____

3. Find the best route between each pair of cities below. Then add the red mileage numbers to figure the distance. Write the mileage.

   Corpus Christi to Dallas _____   Abilene to Brownsville _____

   El Paso to Fort Worth _____   San Antonio to El Paso _____

Reading a Route Map

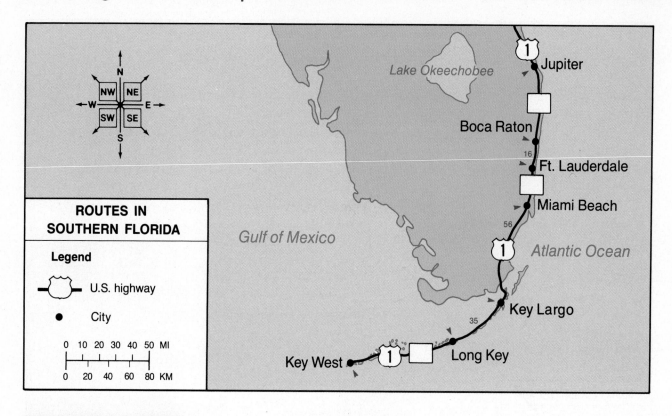

ROUTES IN SOUTHERN FLORIDA

Legend

—⬡— U.S. highway

● City

0 10 20 30 40 50 MI

0 20 40 60 80 KM

MAP ATTACK!

Follow the steps on page 38 to begin reading this map.

1. Some of the red mileage numbers are missing on the map above. Use the map scale to figure the distances between these towns. Choose the closest number from the box below. Then write each distance in the box on the map where it belongs.

   Key West to Long Key

   Jupiter to Boca Raton

   Ft. Lauderdale to Miami Beach

45	35
22	52
71	65

2. What is the distance between Key West and Key Largo? Use the mileage numbers from the map. _____

3. Find Jupiter on the map. Go south on U.S. Highway 1 for 139 miles.

   What city do you reach? _____

4. Continue south on U.S. Highway 1 to Key West. From Jupiter to

   Key West is _____ miles.

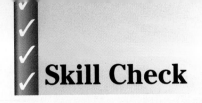

Skill Check

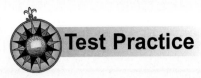
Word Check   route   U.S. highway
                   state highway   interstate highway

1. An _____ crosses the entire country.

2. A _____ connects cities and towns in one state.

3. A _____ passes through more than one state.

4. A _____ is a way of getting from one place to another.

Map Check

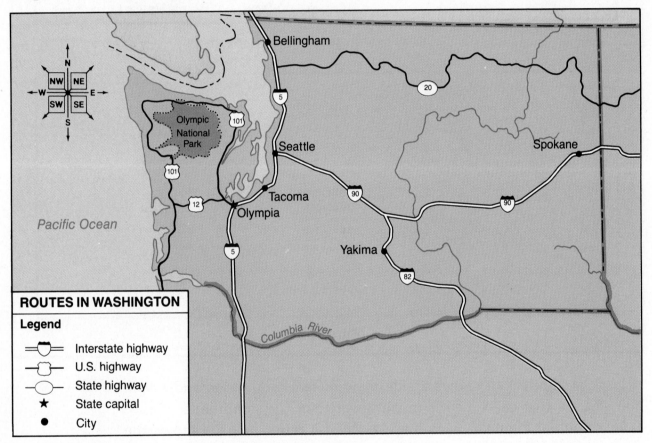

1. What interstate highway passes through Yakima? _____

2. Find Interstate Highway 5. What cities does it pass through?

   _____

3. What U.S. highway goes around Olympic National Park? _____

4. What state highway crosses the northern part of the state? _____

6 Relief Maps

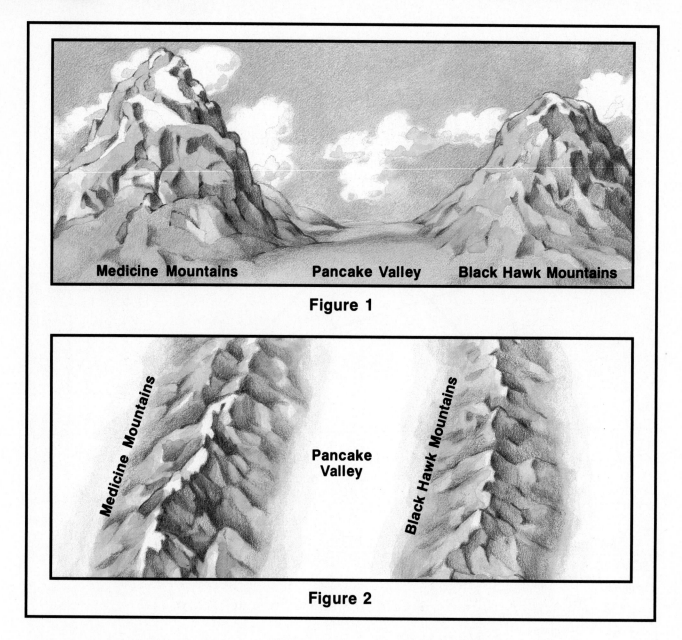

Figure 1

Figure 2

Look at Figure 1. It shows a side view of two mountains and a valley. You can see that the valley is much lower than the mountains.

Now look at Figure 2. This map is called a **relief map**. It shows the same mountains and valley. A relief map has shading to show where the land gets higher and lower. The higher mountains have darker shading. The lower mountains have light shading. The valley has no shading.

▶ Are the Medicine Mountains or the Black Hawk Mountains higher? How do you know?

▶ Which land is lower, the Black Hawk Mountains or Pancake Valley? How do you know?

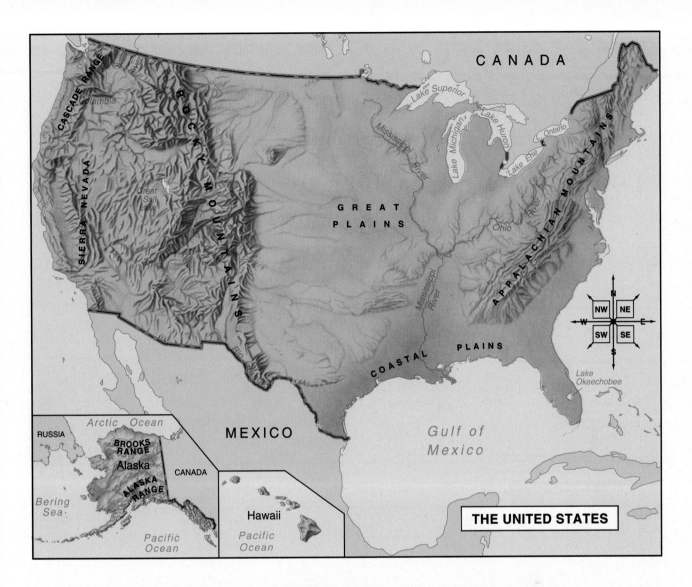

This is a relief map of the United States. On it are mountain ranges, plains, large lakes, and rivers. A **mountain range** is a chain, or group, of mountains. A **plain** is a large area of flat land. Find the Rocky Mountain range on the map. Now find the Great Plains on the map. Which area is darker?

On the map, the mountain ranges have dark shading. The higher the mountains, the darker the shading. The plains have little or no shading.

► Name the mountain ranges on the map.
  Where are they located?

► Which are higher, the Appalachian Mountains or the Rocky Mountains?
  How do you know this?

► Are there more mountains in the eastern or in the western United States?

► Find the Great Plains on the map.
  Name the mountain range west of the Great Plains.

Reading a Relief Map of Alaska

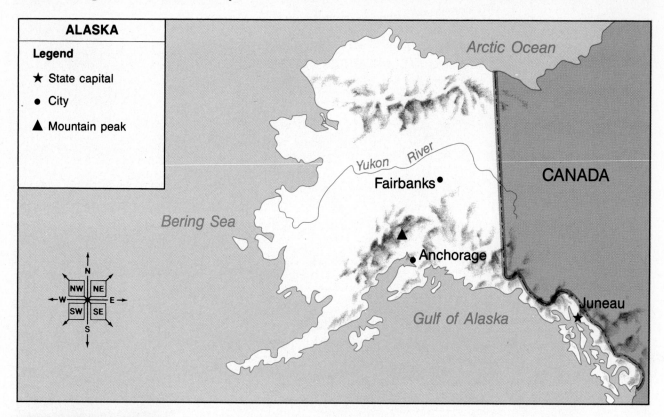

MAP ATTACK!

- **Read the title.** Look at the map. The purpose of this map is to

  show _____.
- **Read the legend.** Check (✔) each symbol in the legend. Check (✔)
  a matching symbol on the map.
- **Read the compass rose.** Circle the intermediate direction arrows.

1. Follow the directions below to finish the map.
   a. Write <u>Brooks Range</u> on the mountain range in northern Alaska.
   b. Write <u>Mt. McKinley</u> near the mountain peak between Anchorage and
      Fairbanks.
   c. Write <u>Coast Range</u> along the southern mountain range near Juneau.
   d. Write <u>Alaska Range</u> on the southern mountain range near Anchorage.

2. What river flows between the Brooks Range and the Alaska Range?

   _____

3. Does the Yukon River run through a valley or a mountain range?

   _____

Reading a Relief Map of the World

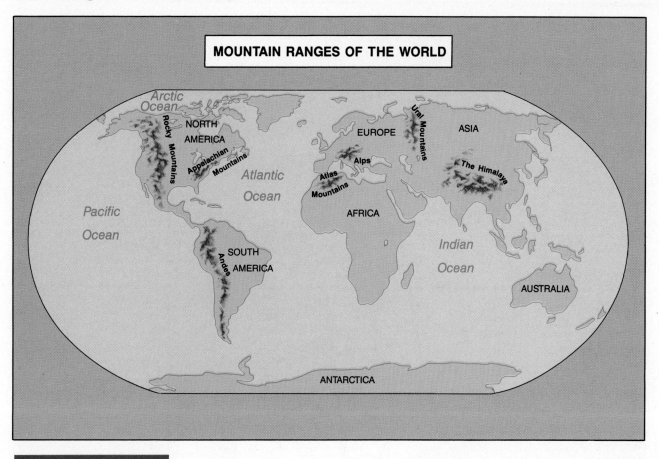

MOUNTAIN RANGES OF THE WORLD

MAP ATTACK!

Follow the first step on page 44 to begin reading this map.

1. Find the seven mountain ranges on the map. Circle the label for each range.
2. Complete this table. Find the continents listed below on the map. Write the name of a mountain range in each continent.

Continent	Mountain Range
North America	_____
South America	_____
Europe	_____
Asia	_____
Africa	_____

Reading a Relief Map of the Western United States

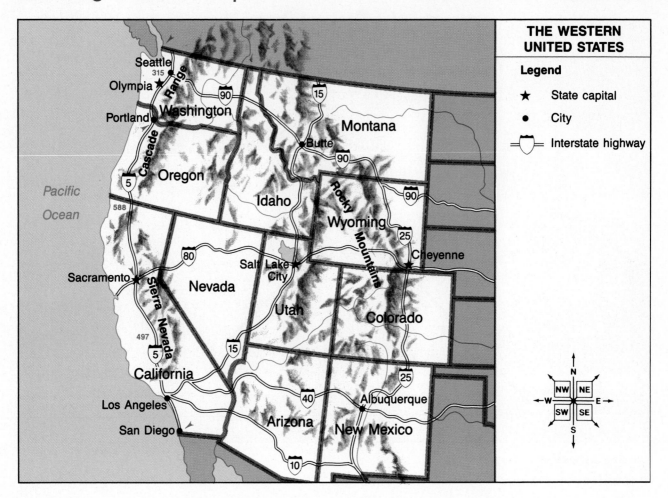

THE WESTERN UNITED STATES

Legend

★ State capital

● City

Interstate highway

1. Locate Interstate 5 on the map. Trace it in red. This interstate runs along the western side of what two mountain ranges?

   _____

2. How long is Interstate 5? Add the red mileage numbers to find the

   distance. Interstate 5 is _____ miles long.

3. Locate the Rocky Mountains on the map. Lightly color them green. What interstate runs along the western side of the Rocky Mountains?

   _____

4. Find Cheyenne, Wyoming on your map. Circle it.

5. Find Interstate 80 going through Cheyenne. Trace Interstate 80 from Cheyenne to Sacramento.

6. What two mountain ranges does Interstate 80 cross?

   _____

Skill Check

Word Check   relief map   mountain range   plain

Write the word that best completes each sentence.

1. A _____ has shading to show where mountains and valleys are.

2. A _____ is a chain of mountains.

3. A _____ is a large flat area of land.

Map Check

1. Follow the directions to label these places on the map.
   a. Write Great Smoky Mountains on the range west of Asheville.
   b. Write Blue Ridge Mountains on the range west of Winston-Salem.
   c. Write Mt. Mitchell on the mountain peak northeast of Asheville.

2. Are the mountains mostly in the east or in the west? _____

Geography Themes Up Close

Regions describe areas that have at least one feature that makes them different from other regions. Geographers organize areas into regions based on their physical features or their human features. For example, geographers might organize the United States into regions based on climate.

The map below shows speech regions in the United States. Most people in the United States speak English. But there are places in the United States where people have certain accents, or ways of pronouncing words. For example, in the New England speech region, people drop the "r" sound from words (*car* is *cah*). In the Southern region, some people add the "r" sound to words so that *wash* sound like *warsh*. The names of some things also differ from speech region to speech region. For example, *flapjacks* or *hot cakes* in the Western speech region are known as *batter cakes* or *crepes* in parts of the Southern speech region. The word for a soft drink is *soda* in some regions and *pop* in other regions. In some places *peanuts* are known as *goobers*.

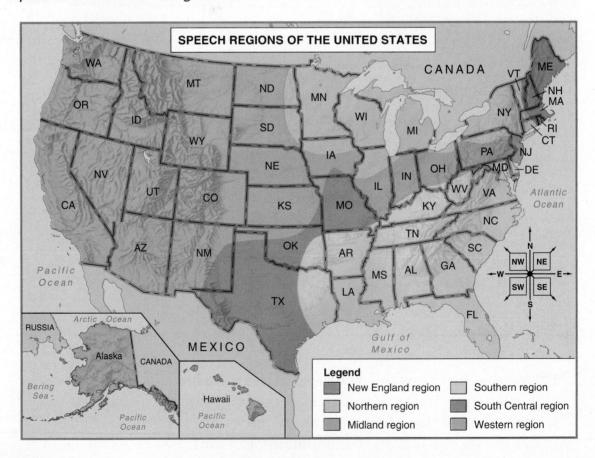

1. What kind of feature—physical or human—describes these regions?

   _____

2. According to the map, which speech region is the largest?

   _____

3. Find approximately where your community is located on the map. Mark it with an **X** on the map. In which speech region is your community?

   _____

4. In parts of Maine and New Hampshire, *pancakes* are called *griddle cakes*. These two states are part of which speech region?

   _____

5. In the Midland region, a *creek* is called a *crick* or a *run*. What states belong to the Midland region?

   _____

   _____

6. Differences in word pronunciation from one part of the country to another are not as noticeable today as they once were. Some differences are disappearing. Why do you think people in different parts of the United States are beginning to speak more alike?

   _____

   _____

   _____

   _____

   _____

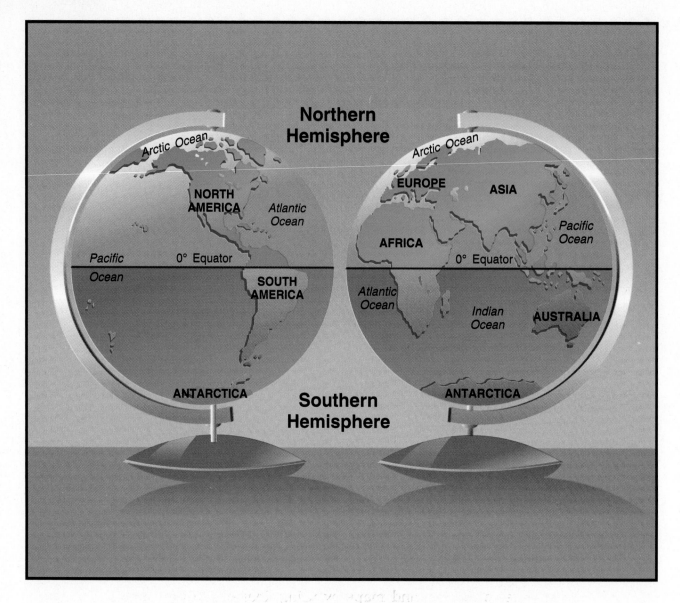

Study each side of the globe in the picture above. Find the dark line that circles the middle of the globe. That line is the **Equator**. The Equator is an imaginary line marked with zero. Find the zero marking the Equator.

The Equator divides the globe into two hemispheres. A **hemisphere** is half the globe. The half of the globe north of the Equator is the **Northern Hemisphere**. The half of the globe south of the Equator is the **Southern Hemisphere**.

► Find North America, Europe, and Asia in the Northern Hemisphere.

► Find Australia and Antarctica in the Southern Hemisphere.

► Trace the Equator with your finger.
What continents and oceans does the Equator cross?

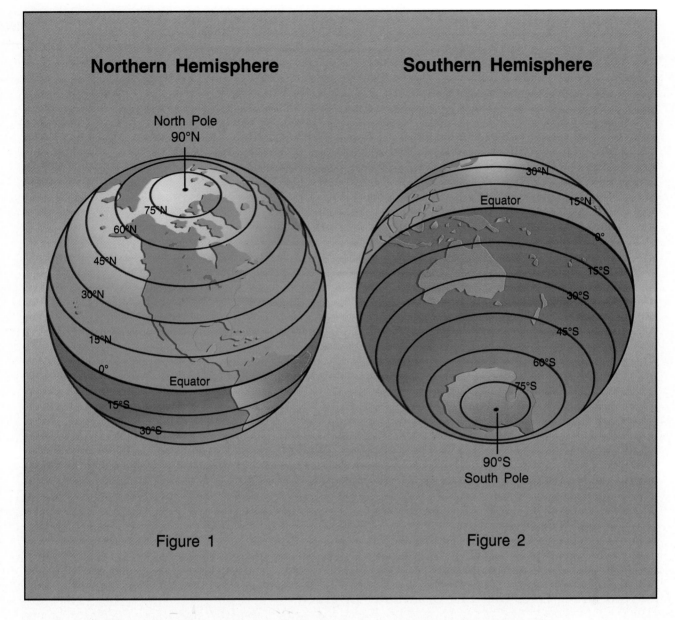

Northern Hemisphere

North Pole
90°N

75°N

60°N

45°N

30°N

15°N

0°

Equator

15°S

30°S

Figure 1

Southern Hemisphere

30°N

Equator

15°N

0°

15°S

30°S

45°S

60°S

75°S

90°S
South Pole

Figure 2

You can find places on globes and maps by using lines of **latitude**. The Equator is the most important line of latitude. The other lines of latitude measure distance north and south of the Equator.

All lines of latitude are numbered. Do you remember that the Equator is marked with a zero? It is 0° latitude. The sign ° stands for **degrees**. The lines that are farther away from the Equator have higher degree numbers. The North Pole is 90° north of the Equator. The South Pole is 90° south of the Equator. The North Pole and the South Pole have the highest degree numbers.

► Find 60° North latitude in Figure 1.
  What continents does it cross?

► Find 15° South latitude in Figure 2.
  What continent does it cross?

Finding Latitude

Degrees of latitude north of the Equator are marked with an N for north. Degrees of latitude south of the Equator are marked with an S for south.

1. Find the Equator. Trace it in red.

   What city lies on the Equator? ___Quito___

2. Find 20°N. Trace that line of latitude in green.

   What city lies at 20°N? ___Mexico City___

3. Find 20°S. Trace that line of latitude in orange.

   What city lies at 20°S? ___Sucre___

4. Find 40°N. Trace that line of latitude in yellow.

   What city lies at 40°N? ___Denver___

5. Find Houston on the map. Circle it in green.
   Houston lies half way between 20°N and 40°N.

   Houston lies on what line of latitude? Make an estimate. ___30°N___

6. Find Lima on the map. Circle it in red.

   Lima lies on what line of latitude? Make an estimate. ___10°S___

Finding Latitude

1. What city lies on the Equator? _Quito_

2. What city lies near 20°S? _Potosí_

3. What city lies at 10°N? _Caracas_

4. What city lies at 40°S? _Valdivia_

5. What city lies between 0° and 10°N? _Paramaribo_

   Estimate its line of latitude. _5°N_

6. What city lies between 20°S and 30°S? _Buenos Aires Asunción_

   Estimate its line of latitude. _28°S_

7. What city lies between 30°S and 40°S? _____

   Estimate its line of latitude. _35°S_

Finding Latitude

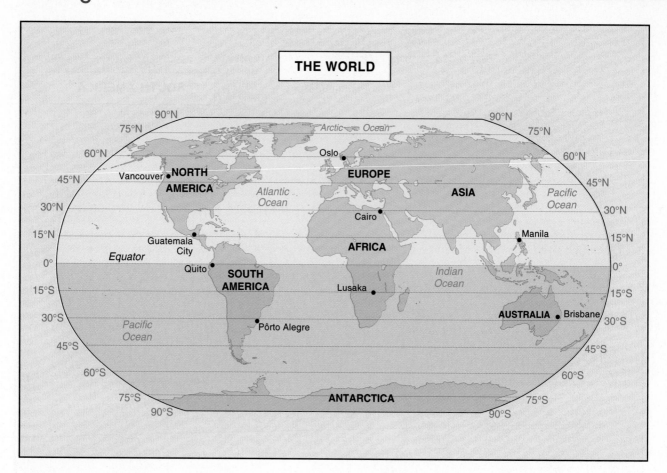

THE WORLD

1. What two cities are at 30°S? _____

2. What two cities are at 15°N? _____

3. What city is at 30°N? _____

4. What city is near 45°N? _____

5. What city is at 60°N? _____

6. What city is at 0°? _____

7. What city is at 15°S? _____

8. 75°S crosses which continent? _____

9. What direction would you go from Guatemala City to Oslo? _____

10. What direction would you go from Cairo to Pôrto Alegre? _____

11. What direction would you go from Manila to Oslo? _____

Skill Check

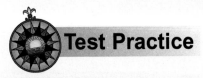

Word Check   latitude   **Northern Hemisphere**
                 Equator **Southern Hemisphere**   **degrees**

1. The _____ is an imaginary line around the middle of Earth.

2. Lines of _____ measure distance north and south of the Equator.

3. Places north of the Equator are in the _____ .

4. Places south of the Equator are in the _____ .

5. Distances on a globe are measured in _____ .

Map Check

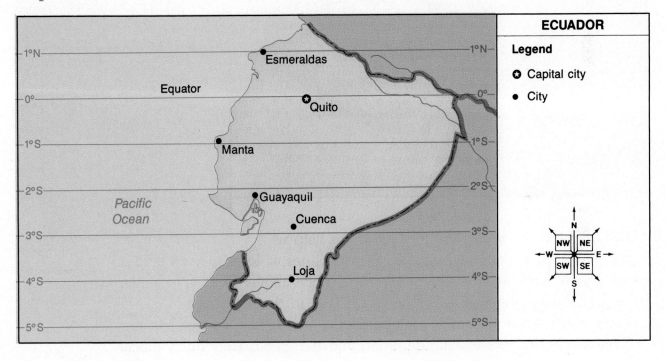

1. Find 1°S. What city lies near 1°S? _____

2. Find 1°N. What city lies at 1°N? _____

3. Find 4°S. What city lies at 4°S? _____

4. Find 2°S. What city lies near 2°S? _____

5. Find 3°S. What city lies near 3°S? _____

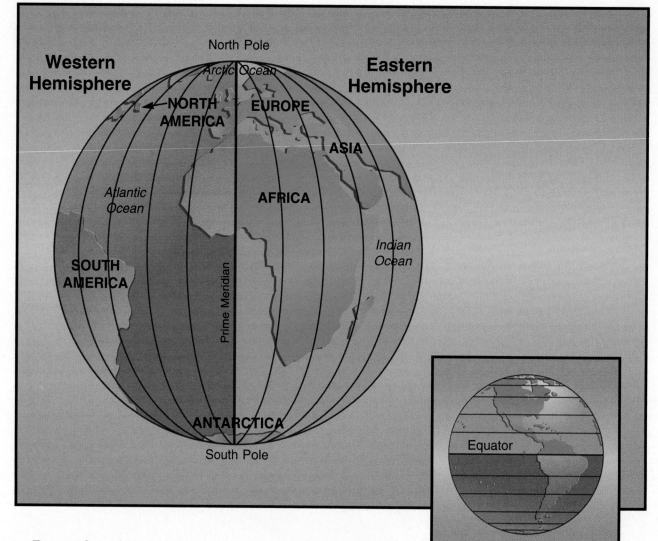

Remember that we use lines of latitude to help us locate places on a globe or map. We also use lines of **longitude** to help us locate places. Look at the large picture of a globe above. With your finger, trace one line of longitude from the North Pole to the South Pole.

Look at the small picture of a globe. Notice that it has lines of latitude.

Remember that lines of latitude go around the globe. They don't touch. Lines of longitude go only halfway around Earth, from the North Pole to the South Pole. Lines of longitude all touch at each Pole.

Lines of longitude are numbered just like lines of latitude. The most important line of longitude is the **Prime Meridian**. The Prime Meridian is 0° longitude.

► Trace the Prime Meridian with your finger.
What continents does the Prime Meridian cross?
What oceans does it cross?

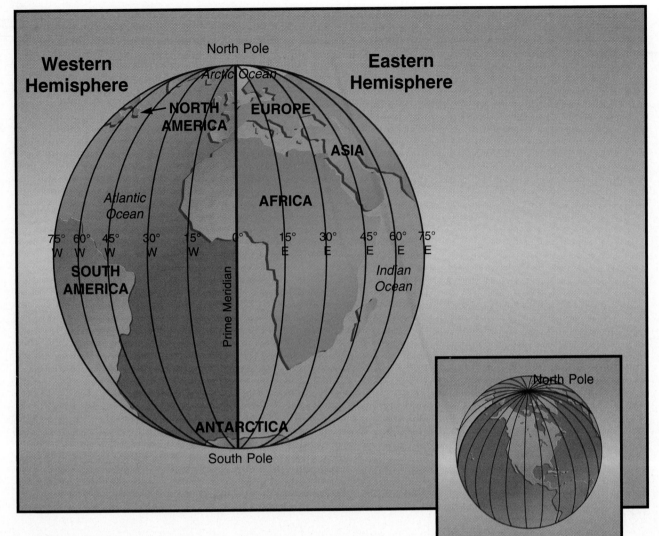

Find the North Pole in the small picture above.
Notice how all the lines of longitude meet at the North Pole. All the
lines of longitude meet at the South Pole too.

Lines of longitude are numbered up to 180°. The 180° line of longitude
and the Prime Meridian form a circle around the globe. That circle
divides the globe into the **Eastern Hemisphere** and the **Western
Hemisphere**. Find the Eastern and the Western Hemispheres in the large
picture above.

Lines of longitude in the Eastern Hemisphere measure distance east of
the Prime Meridian. Lines of longitude in the Western Hemisphere
measure distance west of the Prime Meridian.

► Find 15° West longitude in the large picture.
  What continents does it cross?
  What oceans does it cross?

► Find 30° East longitude.
  What continents does it cross?

Finding Longitude

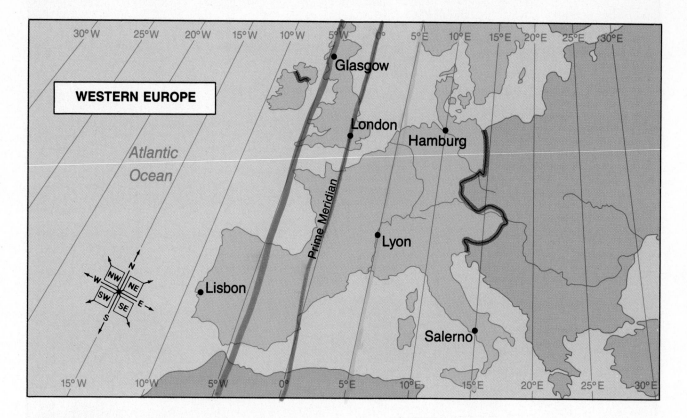

Degrees of longitude east of the Prime Meridian are marked with an *E* for east. Degrees of longitude west of the Prime Meridian are marked with a *W* for west.

1. Find the Prime Meridian. Trace it in red.

   What city lies on the Prime Meridian? __London__ *London*

2. Find 5°W. Trace that line of longitude in green.

   What city lies near 5°W? *glasgow*

3. Find 5°E. Trace that line of longitude in orange.

   What city lies at 5°E? *Lyon*

4. Find 10°E. Trace that line of longitude in yellow.

   What city lies at 10°E? *Hamburg*

5. Find 10°W. Trace that line of longitude in purple.

   What city lies near 10°W? _____

6. Find 15°E. Trace that line of longitude in brown.

   What city lies at 15°E? _____

Finding Longitude

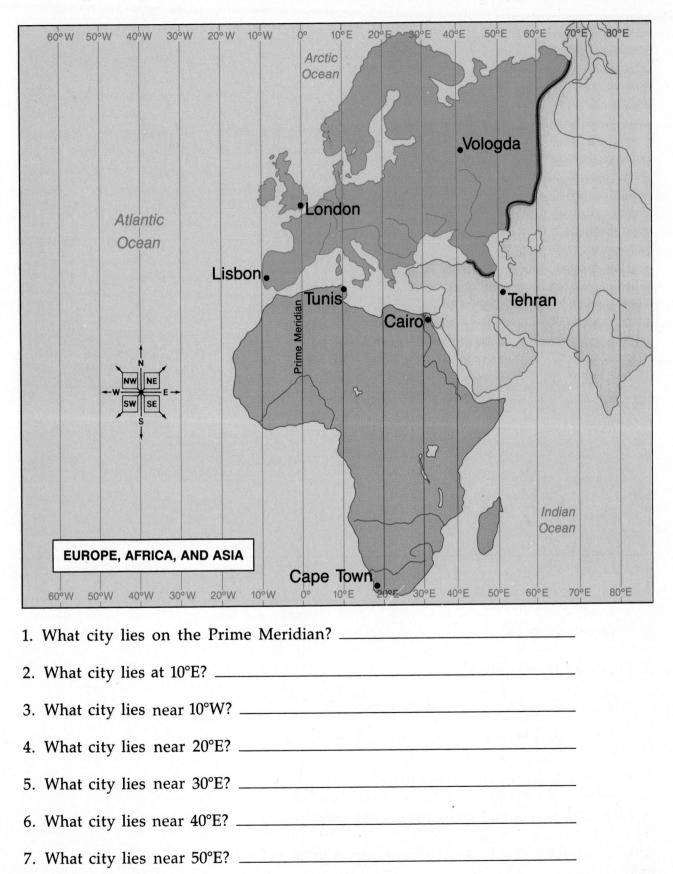

1. What city lies on the Prime Meridian? _____

2. What city lies at 10°E? _____

3. What city lies near 10°W? _____

4. What city lies near 20°E? _____

5. What city lies near 30°E? _____

6. What city lies near 40°E? _____

7. What city lies near 50°E? _____

Finding Longitude

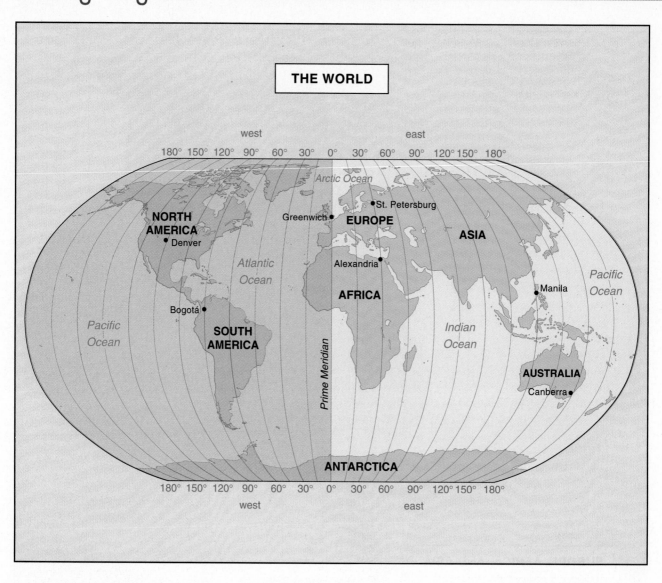

THE WORLD

1. What two cities are at 30°E? _____

2. What city is at 105°W? _____

3. What city is near 120°E? _____

4. What city is at 150°E? _____

5. What city is at 75°W? _____

6. What city is on the Prime Meridian? _____

7. What direction would you go from Alexandria to Canberra? _____

8. What direction would you go from Bogotá to St. Petersburg? _____

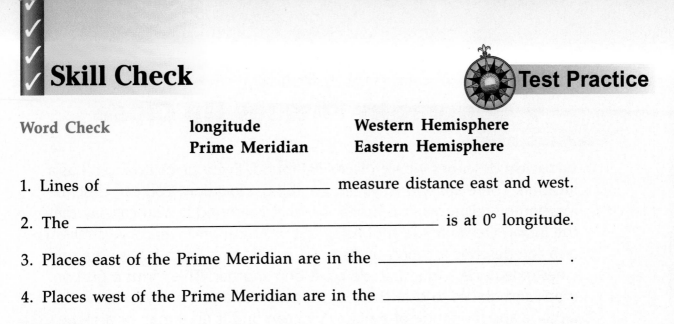

Skill Check

Test Practice

Word Check   **longitude**   **Western Hemisphere**
                     Prime Meridian   **Eastern Hemisphere**

1. Lines of _____ measure distance east and west.

2. The _____ is at 0° longitude.

3. Places east of the Prime Meridian are in the _____ .

4. Places west of the Prime Meridian are in the _____ .

Map Check

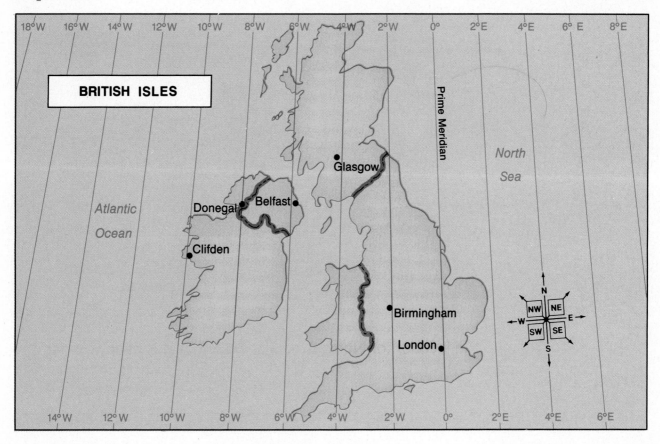

1. Find 2°W. What city lies at 2°W? _____

2. Find 0°. What city lies at 0°? _____

3. Find 6°W. What city lies near 6°W? _____

4. Find 4°W. What city lies near 4°W? _____

5. Find 10°W. What city lies at 10°W? _____

Location describes where places are found. Every place on Earth has a location. There are two ways of describing a location. You can describe location by telling what it is near or what is around it. You can say that the Indian Ocean is south of Asia, east of Africa, and west of Australia. You also can describe location by its exact position on Earth by using a grid. Lines of latitude and longitude cross one another. This forms a grid on maps and globes to give the exact location of a place. If you know the latitude and longitude of a place, you can find it on a map or a globe.

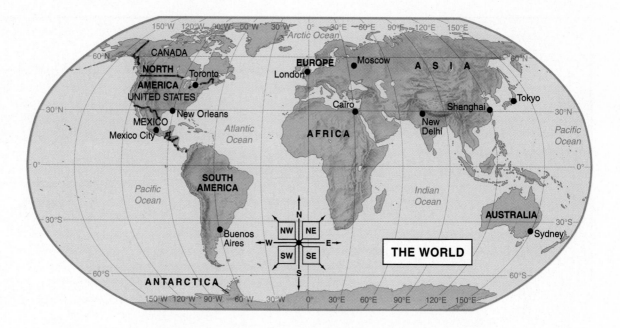

1. Describe the location of North America. Tell what it is near or what is around it.

   _____

   _____

2. Notice on the map that Cairo and New Orleans are located on the same line of latitude—30°N. Find these two cities on the map. Circle them.

3. Cairo and New Orleans, however, are not located at the same place because they are located on different lines of longitude. To give the exact location of a place, you must give both the latitude and the longitude. We say that the exact location of Cairo is 30°N, 30°E. What is the exact location of New Orleans?

_____

4. What is the exact location of Shanghai?

_____

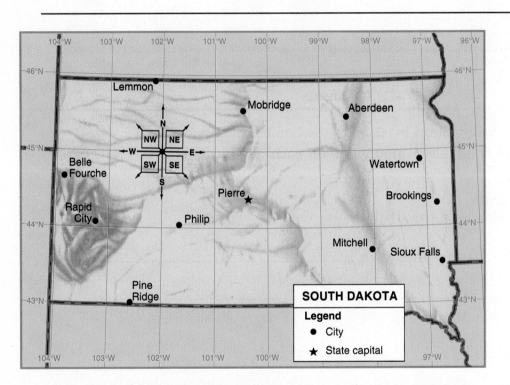

5. Which city in South Dakota is located near 44°N, 100°W?

_____

6. What three cities are located close to 102°W longitude?

_____

7. What is the exact location of Bell Fourche?

_____

9 Graphs

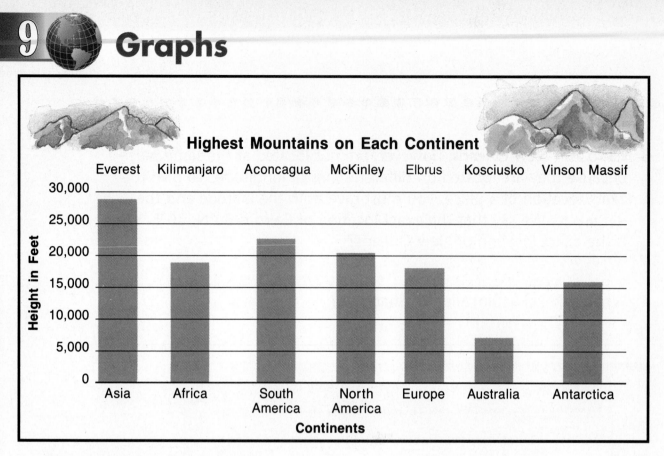

Highest Mountains on Each Continent

Everest   Kilimanjaro   Aconcagua   McKinley   Elbrus   Kosciusko   Vinson Massif

Bar graphs show information by using bars. Some students made a bar graph to compare the highest mountains on each continent.

GRAPH ATTACK!

Follow these steps to read the bar graph.

1. <u>Read the title</u>. This bar graph shows _____

   _____.

2. <u>Read the words at the bottom of the graph</u>. This graph has a colored

   bar for each of seven _____.

3. <u>Read the words and numbers at the left of the graph</u>. The numbers on

   the graph stand for _____.

4. <u>Compare the bars</u>. Read the longest and shortest bars. Put your finger at the top of the bar for Mt. Everest. Slide your finger to the left. Read the number there.

   Mt. Everest is about _____ feet high.

   How high is Mt. Kosciusko? about _____ feet

5. <u>Draw a conclusion</u>. Which continents have the three highest mountains?

   _____

Reading a Bar Graph

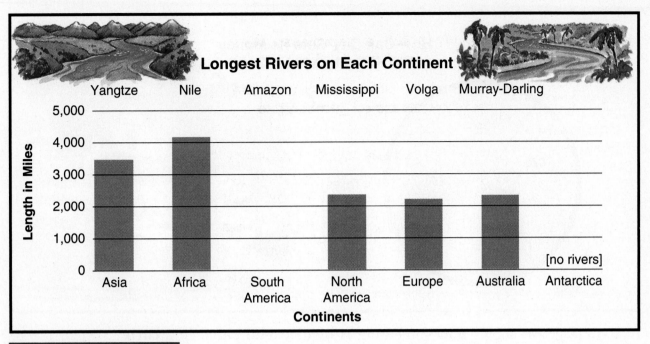

Longest Rivers on Each Continent

Yangtze   Nile   Amazon   Mississippi   Volga   Murray-Darling

GRAPH ATTACK!

Follow these steps to read the bar graph.

1. <u>Read the title.</u> This bar graph shows _____

   _____ .

2. <u>Read the words at the bottom of the graph.</u> The bars on this graph show

   rivers on the _____ .

3. <u>Read the words and numbers at the left of the graph.</u> The numbers on

   this graph stand for _____ .

4. <u>Add to the graph.</u> The Amazon River in South America is 4,000 miles
   long. Add a bar showing the length of the Amazon River.

5. <u>Compare the bars.</u> Read the longest and the shortest bars.

   a. Which continent has the longest river? _____

   b. About how long is it? _____

   c. Which continent has the shortest river? _____

   d. Which continent has no rivers? _____

6. <u>Draw a conclusion.</u> Which three continents have the longest rivers?

   _____

Circle Graphs

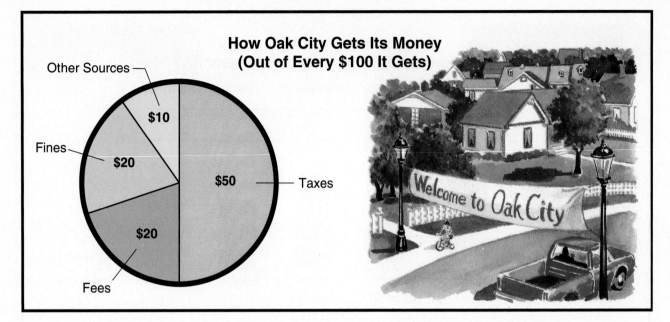

How Oak City Gets Its Money
(Out of Every $100 It Gets)

Other Sources — $10

Fines — $20

$50 — Taxes

$20 — Fees

A **circle graph** shows how something is divided into parts. In a circle graph, the circle stands for the whole. Each part of the circle stands for a part of the whole.

GRAPH ATTACK!

Follow these steps to read the circle graph.

1. Read the title. The whole circle shows _____.

2. Read each part of the circle. What does each part of the circle stand for?

   _____

3. Read the biggest part of the circle. Oak City gets most of its money from

   _____. Out of every $100 it gets, $ ____ comes from this source.

4. Read the smallest part of the circle. Oak City gets the least amount of

   its money from _____. Out of every $100 it gets, $ ____
   comes from this source.

5. Compare the parts of the circle. Use more or less to complete each
   sentence.

   a. Oak City gets _____ of its money from fees than from taxes.

   b. Oak City gets _____ of its money from fines than from other sources.

6. Draw a conclusion. Which two sources are equal? _____

Reading a Circle Graph

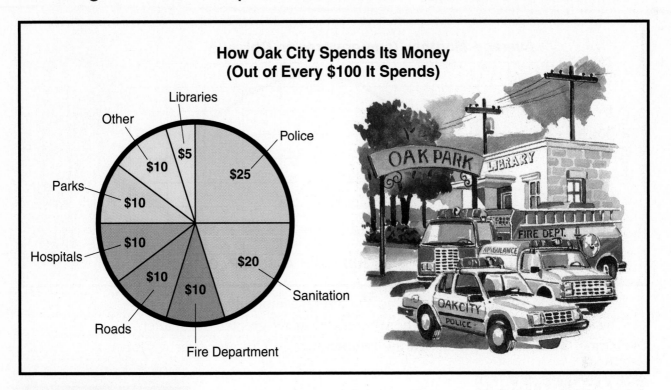

How Oak City Spends Its Money
(Out of Every $100 It Spends)

Libraries
Other
$5
$10
Police
Parks
$10
$25
Hospitals
$10
Roads
$10
$10
$20
Sanitation
Fire Department

GRAPH ATTACK!

Follow these steps to read the circle graph.

1. <u>Read the title.</u> This circle graph shows _____

_____ .

2. <u>Read each part of the circle.</u> Out of every $100 Oak City spends, how

much does it spend on parks? _____

3. <u>Compare the parts of circle.</u> Use <u>more</u> or <u>less</u> in each sentence.

a. Oak City spends _____ money on police than on roads.

b. Oak City spends _____ money on hospitals than on sanitation.
Use <u>largest</u> or <u>smallest</u> in each sentence.

c. Oak City spends the _____ amount of money on libraries.

d. Oak City spends the _____ amount of money on police.

4. <u>Draw a conclusion.</u> Look at the graph on page 66. Does Oak City have
more ways to get money or more ways to spend money?

_____

Line Graphs

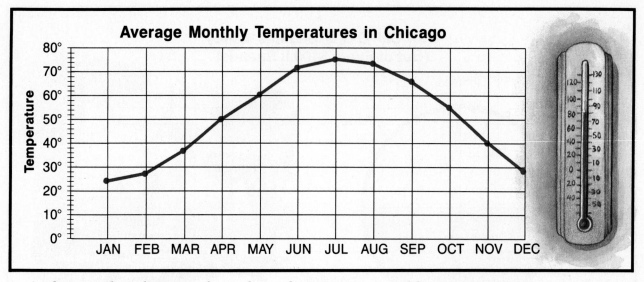

Average Monthly Temperatures in Chicago

A class made a line graph to show the average monthly temperatures in Chicago. A **line graph** shows how numbers grow greater or smaller over time. This line graph shows the temperature in Chicago over a year.

GRAPH ATTACK!

Follow these steps to read a line graph.

1. <u>Read the title.</u> This line graph shows _____.

2. <u>Read the words along the bottom of the graph.</u> This graph shows how

   the temperature changes between _____ and _____.

3. <u>Read the words and numbers on the left side of the graph.</u> These

   numbers stand for _____. The highest number is _____.

4. <u>Read the dots on the line.</u> Put your finger on the dot above January. Slide it to the left to read the temperature.

   In January the average temperature is _____.

   In April the average temperature is _____.

5. <u>Read the shape of the line.</u> Write <u>up</u> or <u>down</u> to complete each sentence.

   From January to July the temperatures go _____.

   From July to December the temperatures go _____.

6. <u>Draw a conclusion.</u> What are the three coldest months in Chicago?

   _____

Reading a Line Graph

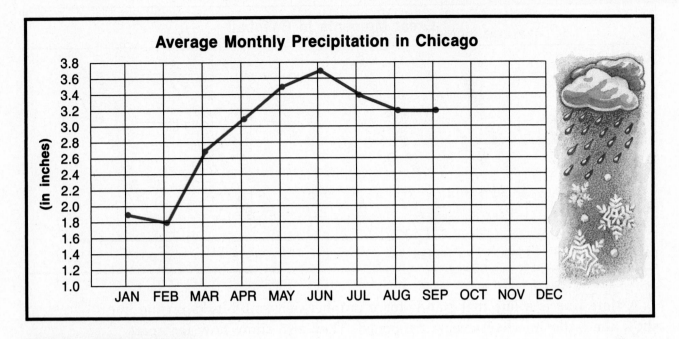

Average Monthly Precipitation in Chicago

(in inches)

JAN FEB MAR APR MAY JUN JUL AUG SEP OCT NOV DEC

GRAPH ATTACK!

Follow the first three steps on page 68 to begin reading this line graph. **Precipitation** is rain and snow.

1. <u>Read the dots on the line.</u> Put your finger on the dot above January. Slide it to the left to read the amount of precipitation.

   In January there were _____ inches of precipitation.

   In April there were _____ inches of precipitation.

2. <u>Finish the graph.</u> Use the information below to add dots to the graph. Then connect the dots to finish the line.

   October 2.6 inches   November 2.3 inches   December 2.1 inches

3. <u>Read the shape of the line.</u> Write <u>up</u> or <u>down</u> to complete each sentence.

   From February to June the amount of precipitation goes _____.

   From September to February the amount of precipitation goes _____.
   The greatest change in precipitation is between what two months?

   _____

4. <u>Draw a conclusion.</u> Compare this graph with the one on page 68. Is there more precipitation in the coldest months or in the hottest months?

   _____

Time Lines

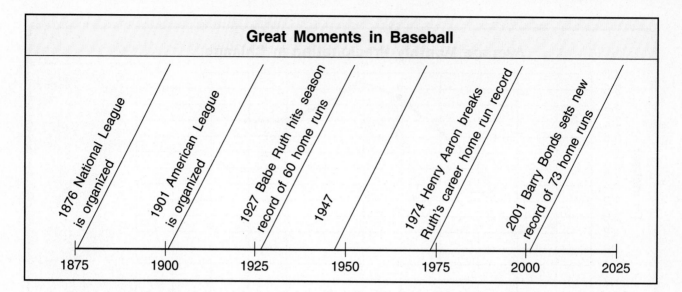

A **time line** is a line that stands for a number of years. Marks on the line show the order in which events happened. They also show how far apart the events are in time. This time line shows great moments in the history of baseball.

TIME LINE ATTACK!

Follow these steps to read the time line.

1. Read the title. This time line shows _____.

   _____

2. Read the dates along the bottom of the time line. This time line begins in

   _____ and ends in _____.

3. Read the time line from left to right.

   What happened in 1876? _____.

   What happened in 1927? _____.

4. Add to the time line. In 1947, Jackie Robinson joined the Brooklyn Dodgers. Write "Jackie Robinson is first black major league player" on the line above 1947.

5. Study the order of events on the time line. Write before or after.

The American League was organized _____ the National League.

Jackie Robinson became the first black major league baseball player _____ Henry Aaron broke Babe Ruth's career home run record.

Reading a Time Line

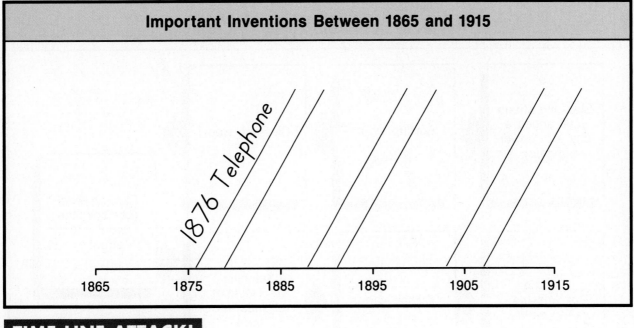

Important Inventions Between 1865 and 1915

1876 Telephone

1865   1875   1885   1895   1905   1915

TIME LINE ATTACK!

Follow the steps to read and finish this time line.

1. <u>Read the title.</u> This time line will show _____

    _____ .

2. <u>Read the dates along the bottom of the time line.</u> This time line

    begins in _____ and ends in _____ .

3. <u>Put the events in order.</u> Read the inventions below. Number them 1
   through 6 in the order they happened.

    _____ 1888 Camera   _____ 1891 Zipper

    _____ 1903 Airplane   _____ 1907 Helicopter

    _____ 1876 Telephone   _____ 1879 Lightbulb

4. <u>Write the events in order on the time line.</u> Write the events in order,
   from left to right on the time line. The first event is written for you.

5. <u>Study the order of events.</u> Write <u>before</u> or <u>after</u>.

    The telephone was invented _____ the zipper.

    The lightbulb was invented _____ the airplane.

    The helicopter was invented _____ the camera.

Flow Charts

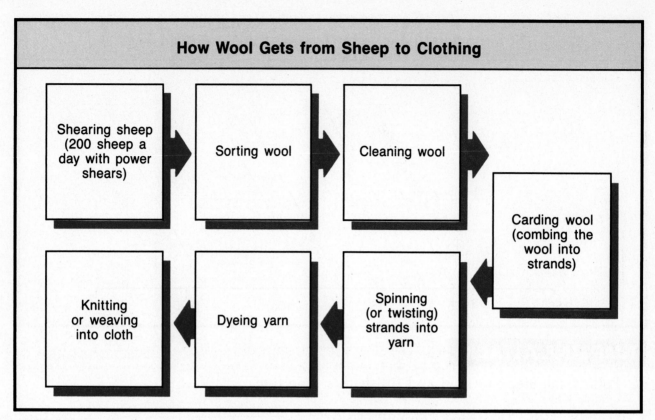

How Wool Gets from Sheep to Clothing

Shearing sheep (200 sheep a day with power shears) → Sorting wool → Cleaning wool → Carding wool (combing the wool into strands) → Spinning (or twisting) strands into yarn → Dyeing yarn → Knitting or weaving into cloth

A class wanted to know how we get clothing from sheep. The teacher made a flow chart to show the steps from sheep to clothing. A **flow chart** is a drawing that shows the steps for doing or making something.

FLOW CHART ATTACK!

Follow these steps to read a flow chart.

1. <u>Read the title.</u> This flow chart shows the steps that explain

_____ .

2. <u>Read the steps.</u> Follow the arrows. This flow chart starts at the top left corner. The first step in getting wool for clothing is

_____ .

The last step is _____ .

3. <u>Study the order of the steps.</u>

Spinning or twisting takes places after _____ .

Before the wool is carded, it has to be _____ and _____ .

Reading a Flow Chart

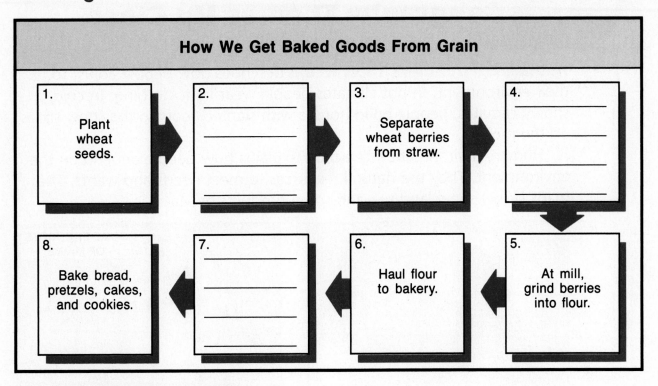

How We Get Baked Goods From Grain

1. Plant wheat seeds.

2. _____

3. Separate wheat berries from straw.

4. _____

5. At mill, grind berries into flour.

6. Haul flour to bakery.

7. _____

8. Bake bread, pretzels, cakes, and cookies.

FLOW CHART ATTACK!

Follow these steps to read and finish the flow chart.

1. <u>Read the title.</u> This flow chart shows how _____

_____

_____.

2. <u>Read the steps.</u> The first step is to _____.

The last step is to _____.

3. Add these missing steps to the flow chart above.
   (2.) Harvest wheat.
   (4.) Haul wheat berries to mill for grinding.
   (7.) Make flour into dough.

4. Study the order of the steps.

Before you haul wheat berries to the mill for grinding, you _____

_____.

After you grind berries into flour, you _____.

Geography Themes Up Close

Human/Environment Interaction describes how people adjust to their environment. In hot climates people wear light clothing. In cold, snowy climates, people build houses with slanted roofs so the snow slides off the roofs.

Human/Environment Interaction explains how people depend on the environment. They use natural resources to meet needs and wants. The maps below show land use and some products of Maine.

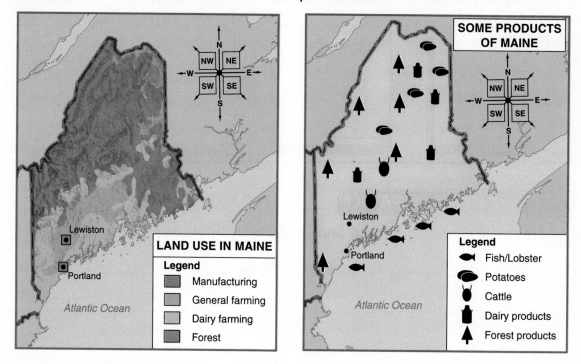

1. How do people use most of the land in southern Maine?

   _____

2. What industry developed along the coast of Maine?

   _____

3. Why would you expect the manufacturing of paper and wood products to be a leading industry in Maine?

   _____

   _____

Human/Environment Interaction explains how people change the environment. When people use the land and its resources to meet their needs, they change the environment. Some changes are good, but some cause problems.

4. Look at the photograph above. How have humans changed the environment? What could result from the changes?

_____

_____

_____

_____

5. How are the people in this photograph trying to change the environment?

_____

_____

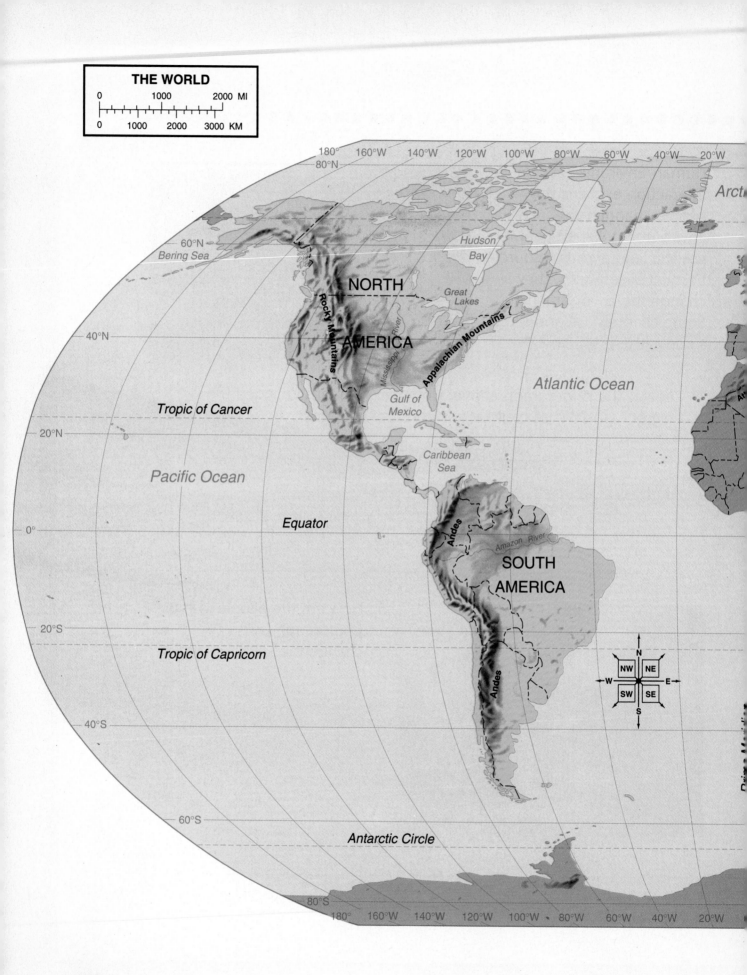

THE WORLD

0   1000   2000 MI

0   1000   2000   3000 KM

180°
80°N
160°W   140°W   120°W   100°W   80°W   60°W   40°W   20°W

Arct

60°N
Bering Sea

Hudson
Bay

NORTH

Great
Lakes

Rocky Mountains

40°N

Appalachian Mountains

AMERICA

Mississippi River

Atlantic Ocean

Tropic of Cancer

Gulf of
Mexico

20°N

Pacific Ocean

Caribbean
Sea

Equator

0°

Andes

Amazon River

SOUTH

AMERICA

20°S

Tropic of Capricorn

N

NW | NE

W ← ⊕ → E

SW | SE

40°S

Andes

S

60°S

Antarctic Circle

80°S
180°   160°W   140°W   120°W   100°W   80°W   60°W   40°W   20°W

Ocean

20°E 40°E 60°E 80°E 100°E 120°E 140°E 160°E 180° 80°N

Arctic Circle

60°N

ASIA

Ural Mountains

Ob
River

Volga River

EUROPE

Alps

Danube
River

Black Sea

Caspian Sea

40°N

Mediterranean Sea

tains

The Himalaya

River River

20°N

Arabian
Sea

Pacific Ocean

AFRICA

River

Red Sea

Ganges River

Nile

Congo River

0°

Indian Ocean

20°S

AUSTRALIA

Great Dividing Range

40°S

60°S

ANTARCTICA

80°S

20°E 40°E 60°E 80°E 100°E 120°E 140°E 160°E 180°

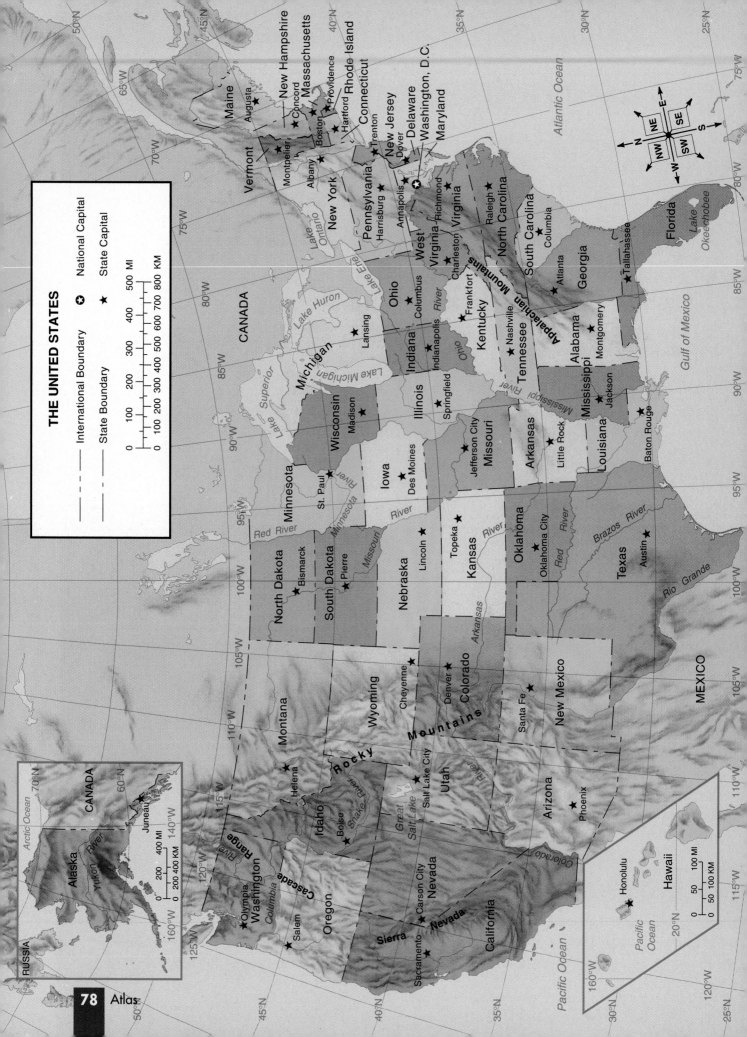

THE UNITED STATES

Legend

✪	National Capital
★	State Capital
– – –	International Boundary
— —	State Boundary

Scale

0 100 200 300 400 500 MI
0 100 200 300 400 500 600 700 800 KM

CANADA

RUSSIA

Alaska

CANADA

Arctic Ocean

Yukon River

Juneau ★

0 200 400 MI
0 200 400 KM

Hawaii

Honolulu ★

Pacific Ocean

0 50 100 MI
0 50 100 KM

MEXICO

Maine
Augusta ★

New Hampshire
Concord ★

Vermont
Montpelier ★

Massachusetts
Boston ★

Rhode Island
Providence ★

Connecticut
Hartford ★

New York
Albany ★

New Jersey
Trenton ★

Delaware
Dover ★

Washington, D.C. ✪

Maryland
Annapolis ★

Pennsylvania
Harrisburg ★

West Virginia
Charleston ★

Virginia
Richmond ★

North Carolina
Raleigh ★

South Carolina
Columbia ★

Ohio
Columbus ★

Kentucky
Frankfort ★

Tennessee
Nashville ★

Georgia
Atlanta ★

Florida
Tallahassee ★

Alabama
Montgomery ★

Mississippi
Jackson ★

Louisiana
Baton Rouge ★

Indiana
Indianapolis ★

Michigan
Lansing ★

Illinois
Springfield ★

Wisconsin
Madison ★

Minnesota
St. Paul ★

Iowa
Des Moines ★

Missouri
Jefferson City ★

Arkansas
Little Rock ★

North Dakota
Bismarck ★

South Dakota
Pierre ★

Nebraska
Lincoln ★

Kansas
Topeka ★

Oklahoma
Oklahoma City ★

Texas
Austin ★

Colorado
Denver ★

Wyoming
Cheyenne ★

New Mexico
Santa Fe ★

Montana
Helena ★

Idaho
Boise ★

Utah
Salt Lake City ★

Arizona
Phoenix ★

Nevada
Carson City ★

California
Sacramento ★

Oregon
Salem ★

Washington
Olympia ★

Lake Superior
Lake Michigan
Lake Huron
Lake Erie
Lake Ontario

Lake Okeechobee

Appalachian Mountains

Rocky Mountains

Cascade Range

Sierra Nevada

Great Salt Lake

Mississippi River
Missouri River
Ohio River
Red River
Minnesota River
Arkansas River
Brazos River
Rio Grande
Colorado River
Snake River
Columbia

Atlantic Ocean
Pacific Ocean
Gulf of Mexico

N NE E SE S SW W NW

Glossary

bar graph (p. 64) a graph with thick lines, or bars, of different lengths to compare numbers or amounts

cardinal directions (p. 8) north, south, east, and west

circle graph (p. 66) a circle that shows how something whole is divided into parts

compass rose (p. 8) a symbol that shows the cardinal and intermediate directions: north, northeast, east, southeast, south, southwest, west, and northwest

continent (p. 45) a very large body of land

degrees (p. 51) the unit of measurement used for lines of latitude and longitude

distance (p. 28) how far one place is from another

Eastern Hemisphere (p. 57) the half of Earth east of the Prime Meridian

environment (p. 5) the surroundings in which a person, animal, or plant lives

Equator (p. 50) the imaginary line around the middle of Earth that divides Earth into the Northern and Southern Hemispheres

flow chart (p. 72) a drawing that shows the steps for doing or making something

hemisphere (p. 50) half the globe; half of Earth; the four hemispheres are Eastern, Western, Northern, and Southern

geography (p. 4) the study of Earth and the ways people live and work on Earth

grid (p. 22) a pattern of lines that cross each other to form squares

human features (pp. 4, 34) features of a place or region made by people, such as buildings, roads, parks, playgrounds, bridges, railroads, farms, factories, and shopping malls

human/environment interaction (pp. 5, 74) the ways people live with and change their environment

intermediate directions (p. 15) northeast, southeast, southwest, northwest

interstate highway (p. 36) a main highway that crosses the entire country

kilometers (p. 28) a unit of length used in measuring distance in the metric system. Kilometers can also be written **KM** and km.

latitude (p. 51) imaginary lines that circle Earth north and south of the Equator. They are numbered and marked by degrees. They are used to locate places.

legend (p. 9) a map key, or list of symbols on a map and what they stand for

line graph (p. 68) a graph that shows how something changes over time

location (pp. 4, 62) where something on Earth is found

longitude (p. 56) imaginary lines that go from the North Pole to the South Pole. They are numbered and marked by degrees. They are used to locate places.

map (p. 9) a drawing of a real place that shows the place from above

map index (p. 23)   the alphabetical list of places on a map with their grid squares

map key (p. 9)   the guide that tells what the symbols on a map stand for

map scale (p. 28)   the guide that tells what the distances on a map stand for

miles (p. 28)   a unit of length used in measuring distance. Miles can also be written **MI** or mi.

mountain range (p. 43)   a chain or group of mountains

movement (pp. 6, 20)   how people, goods, information, and ideas move from place to place through transportation and communication

natural resources (p. 4)   things in nature that people can use, such as water, trees, oil, and gold

Northern Hemisphere (p. 50) the half of Earth north of the Equator

physical features (pp. 4, 34)   features of a place or region formed by nature, such as bodies of water, landforms, climate, natural resources, and plants and animals

place (pp. 4, 34)   tells about the physical and human features of an area that make it different from other areas

plain (p. 43)   a large area of flat land

precipitation (p. 69)   rain and snow

Prime Meridian (p. 56)   the line of longitude running from the South Pole to the North Pole and measured at 0°. It helps divide Earth into the Eastern and Western Hemispheres.

regions (pp. 7, 48)   areas that share one or more features

relief map (p. 42)   a map that shows elevation, or height, of land

resource (p. 10)   things people can use. Some resources are oil, lumber, and water.

route (p. 36)   a road or path from one place to another. Highways, railroads, waterways, and trails are routes.

Southern Hemisphere (p. 50) the half of Earth south of the Equator

state highway (p. 36)   a main road that connects cities and towns within the boundaries of one state

symbol (p. 9)   a picture on a map that stands for something real

time line (p. 70)   a line that shows a number of years and the events that happened in order

title (p. 8)   the name of a map, chart, or graph

U.S. highway (p. 36)   a main highway that passes through more than one state

Western Hemisphere (p. 57) the half of Earth west of the Prime Meridian